Joyful Work in Midlife

The Five Stages

By Dr. Craig Nathanson

Author: How to find RIGHT work during challenging times: A new
approach to your life and work after 40 and other books

Layout and design: Camille Charles, Chamillah Designs

Editing: Natasha Nathanson

Cover art: Camille Charles, Chamillah Designs

Joyful work in Midlife: The five stages by Dr. Craig Nathanson

ISBN-10: 0989668703

ISBN-13: 978-0-9896687-0-5

Library of Congress Control Number: 2013944598

Keywords: Mid-life vocation. Vocational happiness.
Self-awareness in midlife.

Copyright by

Craig Nathanson

2013

ACKNOWLEDGEMENTS

To my wife Natasha who inspires me daily.

Table of Contents

Introduction

This book is an accumulation of twenty years of research, which I have completed in order to understand the factors which influence adults in the middle of their life to pursue greater meaning and purpose in their work and the challenges associated with this path. I have been interested to investigate the experiences of adults who in their midlife identified and followed a new vocational path which better aligned their work with their passions, interests, and abilities. This book explores the path that people went through to find greater fulfillment and meaning in their work.

The key question which frames this research is what is the described experience of midlife adults who change their vocational path to work which has more meaning for them?

In this book, I explore several sub questions:

- How does following a new vocational path in midlife affect one's overall quality of life?

- What challenges do people have when they re-align their interests and abilities and choose to follow a new vocational path in midlife?

- What motivates people to search out or pay attention to

better aligning their vocational interests and abilities in midlife?

- What aspects of life are affected the most when one does the re-alignment of career path in midlife?

While there has been research and much thought given to the topic of midlife and career, I thought there was further opportunity to expand the research around the actual experience of re-aligning one's interests and abilities and following a new vocational path in midlife.

In my own case, I spent years in corporate America living what others would call a successful career filled with big offices, large bonuses, large groups to manage, and an important job title which my mother-in-law could brag about. My doctoral studies began in the fall of 1993. During that time, I was at the highest point of my corporate career. I had a senior management role in the most profitable company in the world at the time, many material acquisitions, and a developing family. Despite this external view, I was empty internally. Deep inside, I had this angst and even more, deep depression. I didn't enjoy my work of managing. It seemed repetitive and only aimed at making money for the larger enterprise of which I was just a small mechanism in their big system. I wanted to express myself in my work, in ways which I could see made a real difference in the world. The problem was that I didn't know what to do, how to express this, or even where to start. I did know most of the time I just wanted to run away, to be high on a mountain, alone to figure this out. I also noticed one important thing, that there was not much support around me to make any sort of change at this point of my life. My work didn't bring joy or passion. I felt that I had accomplished what society had expected up to this point of my life at the ripe age of 37. I began to notice how my co-workers seem to go about their work days like robots. At this point, I thought that by starting a PhD program I could begin to unravel this sense of feeling lost at the start of my mid-life period and perhaps in the process help others as well.

My major transition from senior manager in a Fortune 50 company to a new life as a teacher, speaker, writer, and coach took great risk and courage while shutting down external voices and opinions. I knew at the start of my transition that whatever might result would never be as bad as staying with what I was doing: a work life of incoherence, insignificance, and emptiness. This transition was a catalyst to shed other areas of my life which were holding me back. I moved forward, went through divorce after 23 years of unhappy marriage, bankruptcy, house foreclosure, and moved my kids and I into a 400-square-foot apartment. At last I was free. This was the biggest, boldest move I had ever made in my life. It wasn't easy. Looking back now after a new marriage and happiness I have acquired in my personal and work life, I can see that this step into the unknown was a necessary step for making much needed change in my life.

This book and my research has potential benefits for people in midlife who find themselves burned out, in transition, laid off, or unsatisfied in what they currently do. Midlife is a time of anxiety and inner turmoil for many adults. Since work takes up a significant amount of people's daily activities, in many cases adults start asking themselves questions about the work they do and its meaning. Therefore, Joyful work in midlife: The five stages will provide ideas and reflection on the path and steps for those seeking fulfilling work in midlife.

The Objective of this Book

There have been many ideas written in the last 100 years about work and the challenges of work at midlife. My objective of this book is to cover some of the history of how work has been perceived by others. At the same time I want to give you my own perspective from my journey and research over the past twenty years which began when first I started to question my own work and its meaning. I also will show how to make sense of what to do next!

Midlife and its Relationship to Work

Midlife stages and the relationship to work have been gaining interest in recent years. Researchers have coined different terms for this stage such as "the third age," or "third chapter" (Lawrence-Lightfoot, 2009). In this third chapter, new possibilities are emerged and turned into opportunities. This period has also been called "middleescence" (Dychtwald & Kadlec, 2009). The notion of staying engaged longer opens up a new stage of life for pursuing new interests and passions.

Some researchers have described this period as "Act IV," or "a five-act course" (Carstensen, 2009). This new Act IV lacks social benchmarks about what should be done and how with regard to work, sex, and relationships. For example, a study of midlife women going through career transition revealed that relations with partners were instrumental in the success of these transitions (Motulsky, 2010). In this modern era the mid-life career and the issue of having meaning in the workplace becomes more important. According to the Department of Health and Human Services (2011) the average age of the older population grows and expected to grow 19% by 2030. In the next 20 years, one out of four Americans will be over age 65. Where does that place you?

Mid-life change has different impact and meaning for different people. Women have different challenges than men (Emslie & Hunt, 2009). Many popular authors (Goldman, 2009; Roach, 2011; Sheehy, 1995) have described the unique changes which women go through during their middle years. Faced with sexual challenges, changes in their role in the family, internal struggles for independence, women seek out their own ways to have meaning in midlife, the ways which lead them to a better understanding of their true self. Other authors discussed the importance of active engagement for women and men in midlife (Bateson, 2010; Lawrence-Lightfoot, 2009). Midlife and career choices are often more challenging for those who have been imprisoned, homeless, disabled, or caught in severe discriminatory situations (Chope, 2006). The age of active wisdom, or Adulthood II (Bateson, 2010), is a new opportunity for midlife adults to reinvent themselves. This period of life is a great opportunity for finding ways to adapt, explore, and channel one's energies, skills, and passions (Lawrence-Lightfoot, 2009).

Take a moment and reflect. What are your own challenges about your work and life? What are some goals which you have which are most important? Keep these in mind as you read this book. You will find the keys which will open the right doors for you.

Levinson (1978) said that midlife is a period when one starts questioning what was accomplished. Individuals in midlife start to question their contributions to society measured against society expectations and their own expectations for this period in their lives. Some individuals deal with the disparity between where they are and where they dreamed they would be. What questions do you have now about your life? Don't be afraid to ask them. This will lead towards the path which is just right for you.

Many people in midlife take stock of reappraising their life and restructuring some of these areas (Jung, 1959). "Wholly unprepared, they embark upon the second half of life when we take the step into the afternoon of life; worse still we take this step with the false assumption that our truths and ideals will serve as before" (Welch, 1982, p. 95).

Change becomes necessary in midlife often as a result of loss a spouse or a job (Roach, 2011; Sheehy, 1995). Some adults in midlife experience episodes of self-appraisal and instinctual awakening (Vaillant & McArthur, 1972). At the same time, these mid-life adults crystallize their concerns as a tendency toward the existential questioning of self-values and life itself (Gould, 1972). What changes have you been through recently? How have you dealt with these changes?

Many people in midlife realize the fact that they are no longer young. This generates an awareness of who they are, what they have done, and where they might be going (Bardwick, 1986). Some people experience bodily decline and a vivid recognition of their mortality, which also raise new concerns in midlife (Levinson, 1978). Others report feeling low levels of energy for life itself (Tamir, 1989). For many people, the experience of midlife involves a curious blend of resurgence and decline (McAdams, Josselson, & Lieblich, 2006). I have found that in midlife it can be easy to spend too much time looking backwards. It is far better to take the time and invest new thinking into new possibilities for work and life in the second half.

Lambley (1995) suggested that mid-life work success or reaching a plateau in career creates circumstances that allow people to re-evaluate their life and career status. In my own life I noticed that this inner questioning is healthy though at times difficult.

These questions around one's job and more importantly whether they continue to be interested in a current job provide a sort of test for the ability to cope with change in midlife. Some individuals, when faced with additional work start to wonder if it is all worth it and start to question their roles. Others ask the most important question of all: what our soul asks of us (Hollis, 2003). As a result of this questioning, their autonomous development is stunted if they feel as though work is no longer worth the effort or when work demands don't align to what they want to do (Chalofsky, 2010).

Some individuals in midlife start wondering about life outside of their traditional work environment. Have you? People wonder how they would actually spend their day if they had unlimited flexibility and opportunity (Reisman, 1961). For some people, the passion that has driven them to engage in their worlds of work becomes subject to a deeper review of what they really want. People in midlife become choosier in how they plan to expend their psychic energy (McAdams, Josselson, & Lieblich, 2006). Hudson (1995) said that in midlife people become more complete persons. At this point of life they are able to conduct an audit of their lives to review current personal commitments, while simplifying and deepening key relationships.

If you were right now to conduct your own audit of your life, what would you find? Many people have neglected their psychological needs until midlife when suddenly these needs rise to the surface (Lambley, 1995). Perhaps you have seen these people at work. They work as robots rarely smiling going about their day in a mechanical way without joy or passion. They go home and the next day is more of the same. On a scale of 1-10 with 1 being terrible and 10 being amazing, what score would you give yourself and your normal work day?

Mid-Life Crisis

Midlife feels like a crisis to many (Edwards, 2008; Gould, 1972; Vaillant, 1977). Much of the phenomenon suggests that for some individuals the sense of crisis is greater than for others (Tamir, 1989). Some people face a crisis or wait for the crisis to come (Hollis, 2001). For others, midlife is the greatest period of life full of greater happiness, productivity, community involvement, as well as increased feelings of well-being (MacArthur Foundation, 2012). In fact, the upheaval may be an exception rather than the rule.

It is difficult to experience a mid-life conflict if one does not take the time to figure out how to come to grips with life and embrace the fact that one is getting older (Raines, 1994). It is necessary in midlife to move aside ego and to discover if there is a deeper force within that calls (Hollis, 2003). Midlife drives a sudden need to transition to something else (Lewin, 1935). Many adults in midlife have similar patterns of deceleration and disengagement with present situations, which causes a shift in thinking and sense of being in mental transition. As a result, some people may suddenly feel burnt-out, depressed, and constricted on the job (Hall & Rabinowitz, 2008). The periods of deceleration and disengagement are also described as events in which an individual experiences a personal discontinuity and must develop new assumptions or behavioral responses because the situation is new or the required behavioral adjustments are novel (Brammer & Abrego, 1981). These patterns suggest that mid-life transition is a time of both growth and confusion. It may also be a time to repair wounds of the soul, our inner life (Hollis, 2006). The mid-life transition is described as a deeply human experience. Even midlife psychologists state that "the popular notion of a 'midlife crisis' as a normative developmental experience" has been "overdramatized" (Reid & Willis, 1999).

As noted by Brehony (1996), some of us drift in it barely noticing the effects, while for others it feels as a disaster. The critical success factor is when one shows the ability to question the existing structure and search for new possibilities in the world.

I found that for many people this is hard to do as we become stuck in our cycles of doing the same activities over and over without questioning their value. How about you? Which things in your life and work have become routine and now lack deeper meaning for you?

Several authors have described similar cycles of change in midlife (Edwards, 2008; Erikson, 1959; Fiske, 1980; Jung, 1954; Neugarten, 1968). This period of life for many is a time of change and personal transformation while risks of depression and rigidity may clash with opportunities for greater integration and personal growth (Jung, 1954).

For some adults, arriving at the brink of midlife feels like being stranded in a foreign country (Mayer, 1978). Suddenly, the realization of risks not taken, chances ignored, and the sudden clarity of getting older causes many to face an unprepared future (Goldman, 2009; Lawrence-Lightfoot, 2009; Roach, 2011; Sheehy, 1995).

Self-Reflection in Midlife

Some people feel content for the majority of their working life if their situation meets externally viable needs and they are rewarded properly. Many assume that rewards follow correct behavior if they are willing to sacrifice for success. For example, individuals expect that if they do their part, life will pay off accordingly (Gould, 1972). Many of us, while in midlife, start to question the value and purpose of work. This is why it's important in midlife to consider not only the values but also the degree of fit between the individual and the current work environment (Levinson, 1978). In midlife, some people discover during self-reflection that their current work situation is not suitable, as it does not allow them to carry out important aspects of themselves (Roach, 2011; Browning, 2007).

Is there a part of you which is not being fulfilled and is crying out for attention now? This is important to pay attention to. Many mid-life adults pay a price when the vision of their life does not match internal expectations. Many people remain in jobs for many years feeling empty while doing work, which is of little importance to them. This pattern can continue until a combination of external pressure and inner readiness emerges. This inner readiness leads to self-reflection in midlife. Some people start to ask themselves deep questions about the value of their life and their contribution to society. This is healthy. What questions can you ask yourself about your own life now? Others seek for more meaning in their work as they are meaning-seeking creatures (Hollis, 2006). Most important, however, is the realization that there might be a gap between where they expected to be and where they are now. This tension is inherent in the human condition and therefore is indispensable to mental well-being (Frankl, 1984).

Ignoring Inner Needs in Midlife

I have observed that people tend to avoid activities which prevent them from dealing with the deeper issues about their work in midlife. Sometimes people are reluctant about sharing the things which matter most. Some adults in midlife carry around the symbols of their self-worth in their consciousness (Becker, 1971). The symbols like a big house, fancy car, or expensive clothes can give them an artificial sense of self-worth. Many adults in midlife, however, feel competent and satisfied in their work (Evans & Bartolome, 1986). While they may not feel contented, they are challenged enough so that they are not driven to change by negative thoughts and emotions.

Once individuals experience failure in reaching their personal goals it is easy to have their self-worth damaged. If the fear of this failure is greater than change itself, it is possible that those individuals will not be able to make the required changes in midlife that are required for renewal and growth (Bardwick, 1986). Levoy (1997) suggests that some people in midlife are afraid to follow their true passions as they might be called "crazy" by others. This influences their sense of self-worth, which is seriously impaired based on the external feedback. Those individuals who are considered normal in terms of being well adapted are often less healthy than some neurotic individuals in terms of human values. Often they are well adapted only at the expense of having given up themselves in order to meet the external expectations. All genuine individuality and spontaneity may have been lost at this point (Fromm, 1941).

Historical Views on Work Nature

A brief historical review may help to understand how certain patterns of thinking about the nature of work have emerged over the years. The word "job" dates back to the renaissance. Originally called "gob," it related to a small piece, any task or single piece of work. Early workers were piece-workers (Halberstam, 2000). The word "career" derived from the French word "carrier" which was defined as a racing course or road. Later, it was defined as one's progress through life or in a particular vocation or along some specific course.

Religion played a historic influence in the nature of work. Economic exploitation meant the use of people labor, which produced alienation, bad feeling, and was thought of as false consciousness. Early, Christians viewed work as an opportunity to help those less fortunate by sharing their fruits of labor. Idleness was viewed as a kin to sinfulness. Martin Luther (1913), in the 16th century, viewed work as a form of serving God and believed it was important to perform to one's ability, which was equal to one's spiritual value. Marx (1963), as the founder of the modern critique of alienated labor, viewed that alienation occurs when a person lost the ability to direct the part of his or her life which was invested in work. Marx posited that those who were forced to sell their labor to those who owned the means to production became alienated from their work. Other early thinkers placed equal thought on the importance of work to an individual's sense of self (Dewey, 1933; Freud, 1914) and later (Sarason, 1977). Little emphasis on the re-examination of work and what one does was discussed much by the above early thinkers.

Theories of Career Development

The career theory in its development has focused on systematic methods to help people identify their vocational paths. Historical patterns helped contribute to modern-day thinking about work in both positive and negative terms. Thus, it is important to examine what the major career influencing models were. Multiple views and perspectives drive present career theory. The most influential theories are trait and factor theory, life stage theory, social cognitive theory, decision making theory, developmental theories, and organizationally based theories. Trait and factor theory (Holland, 1997; Parsons, 1909; Patton & McMahon, 2006; Patterson & Darley, 1936; Rounds, 1990; Williamson, 1939) focuses on individual measurable traits (for example, interests and abilities) and matching them with similar occupation. Trait and Factor theory, similar to other career development process models, emerged from an early emphasis on multiple steps: analysis, syntheses, diagnosis, prognosis, and counseling.

Early work in this area paved the way for the start of vocational schools (Brewer, 1922) and the general acceptance that understanding one's self consisted of understanding one's abilities, aptitudes, interests, and limitations. Trait and factor theory researchers suggested that each person had unique patterns and traits and therefore by closely matching them with vocations, productivity growth could be increased. They focused more on individual outputs vs. general happiness, fulfillment and greater meaning within the work environment. Many researchers thought that Trait and factor theory was too rigid and no longer as viable as originally thought (Patton & McMahon, 2006; Rodgers, 1961; Rounds, 1990).

Again, little thought was discussed in early research around the re-examination of one's work as a person ages. The client centered methods of Rodgers (1961) provided an alternative approach to other fields such as career development. Despite the success of Rodgers and his views, trait and factor theory continues to be the foundation for the majority of career counseling and approaches today (Patton & McMahon, 2006). Several variations of the trait and factor theory emerged which focused on differences in personality types as they related to vocation (Holland, 1997). Holland based his model on the assumption that vocational satisfaction and stability and achievement depended on congruence between personality and one's environment. This became a simple model for many people to adopt. Unfortunately, it took most of the thinking and inner reflection out of the equation for following one's vocation.

How about you? How did you end up in the career you have now? Earlier researchers sought to define theory which placed the importance not on assessments but on the life roles and choices one made in one's occupational careers, (Miller & Form 1951; Osipow, 1969). Other sociological perspectives (Gottfredson, 1982; Miller & Form, 1951) suggest that men and women tend to differ in occupational aspirations and, in fact, make career choices as an attempt to place one's self in the broader social order. Career theorists for many years have ignored the issues of career development of different ethnic and cultural minority groups. Different cultural values play a significant role in career choices along with other factors (Ibrahim, Ohnishi, & Wilson, 1994).

Super (1990), in his life stage theory sought to combine different approaches which integrated developmental, differential, social, and phenomenological ways of knowing. Life stage theory suggested that while abilities and interests drove vocational choices, they could evolve over time based on how life roles fluctuated.

Social cognitive theory assumes that cognitive factors play a key role in career development and career decision-making (Lent & Brown, 2011). Cognitive factors include self-efficacy, outcome expectations, and personal goals. This theory is a prevailing model in career counseling approaches today (Mitchell & Krumboltz, 1996). Social cognitive theory provides a unifying framework for linking together vocational interests, making work related choices and achieving career success (Lent & Brown, 2008).

Social cognitive ideas are closely linked to the decision making theory (Heppner & Krauskopf, 1987; Tiedeman & O'Hara, 1963), which suggests that career development is a continuous process marked by key decision points. In the case of vocation, instead of making one single specific vocational choice early in one's career, decision-making skills are used to evaluate a whole range of options and career options. Additionally, career decision making and indecision have a close linkage to psychological and social cognitive factors (Shoffner, 2011).

This is in contrast to the trait and factor theory which doesn't take into account external events which could alter one's vocational choices regardless of vocational or personality predisposition. The trait and factor theory of career development goes back to the 1900s and is associated with vocational theorists Frank Parsons (1909) and E.G. Williamson (1939). The basic assumption of this theory is that each person has a unique pattern of traits of interests, values, abilities, and personality characteristics. Every occupation consists of factors required for the successful performance of that occupation. It is possible to identify a fit or match between individual traits and job factors. The closer the match between personal traits and job factors the greater the possibility for successful job performance and satisfaction.

Other career development theories suggested that career decision-making was linked to one's internal psychological needs or values (Allport, Vernon, and Lindsey, 1960; Roe, 1956). Additionally, the importance of values served as a standard by which people evaluated their actions (Brown, 2002; Super, 1953). This approach of career development suggested that values are driven by beliefs, which contain cognitive, affective, and behavioral dimensions.

Midlife is a New Era of the Meaning of Work

Work has been labeled as having three components: significance, orientation (goals and objectives), and coherence (inner life congruence) (Morin, 1995). Still as we reach the middle age of our work lives, I have observed that we start to ask deeper questions to ourselves whether the work we are doing still makes sense and holds meaning for us. For example, ask yourself right now, does your work give you meaning, make sense to you? If no, then new questions and action are needed now!

The meaning of work global study (MOW Int'l Research Team, 1987) was focused on understanding how adults view their work, and it concluded that two out of three individuals have a strong attachment to working as a way of life. Eighty-six percent said they would continue working even if they had enough income. This is even more important today as people are living and working longer than ever before in history. In 1900, the life span in the United States was 47. Today, according to the U.S. Census Bureau (2012), adults in the US are expected to live well into their 70s. How long do you expect to work? I suggest you plan to work the rest of your life. Why? When we work at what we enjoy, we live an authentic life filled with purpose and meaning. But this work life should be designed by you! Which work could you do forever which you love and find passion in?

In the meaning of work global study (MOW Int'l Research Team, 1987), having interesting work was the priority for people. In my own research, I wanted to understand what the experiences have been for mid-life adults who have followed a more meaningful path to their work.

Unfortunately, for some people, work represents activities that have been left over like crumbs after all the managerial and satisfying aspects have been taken away (Sievers, 1986). Cochran (1990) has defined work not as a means but as an end itself as an auto-telic activity. A person can leave interesting work for another job, but one cannot leave the world of work without a radical change in one's sense of personhood. Meaning of work defines the difference between self -directed and other-directed work (Halberstam, 2000). When self-directed, our work defines our own choices and reflects our values and fits how we wish to work with an appropriate degree of input from others. Other-directed work is labor where one is constrained and one's work doesn't fit one's goals or values. Some organizations overemphasize people skills and experience while ignoring other factors such as personality and individual goals (Evans & Bartolome, 1981). At the very least, this can lead to internal tension and overwork. Additionally, administrators in some organizations misunderstand and frankly don't care how meaning occurs in work, leading to motivational strategies which underemphasize the context (Pinder, 1984).

These days so many organizations place profit above people so it becomes easy for people to feel like they are in job prison. I doubt you will ever see an HR professional come up to you on Monday morning and ask you if you are finding joy in your work!

As a result, this may prevent people from re-examining their work and their current paths. This may also influence or make it difficult for adults in midlife to recognize that something is missing in their work-related activities. This study is interested in discovering what the experiences of adults were who did recognize a gap and took action to better align their work- related lives. Is there something missing for you in your work life?

The Lack of Meaning at Work

Many organizations confuse motivation with meaning and believe if their workers are motivated, then their work must have meaning (Robin, 1998). Many workers are afraid of failure and continue to work harder at jobs which have no meaning (Evans & Bartolome, 1981). This overemphasis on productivity and sense of doing things which are not personally rewarding contributes towards inner conflict (Handy, 1991; Handy, 1999; Halberstam, 2000; Morin, 1995; Terkel, 1975). Organizational life has been criticized for its failure to find ways to restore meaning and better align workers to their capabilities and individual needs and desires (Sievers, 1986; Sarason, 1977). Some of this thinking can be traced back to the turn of the century management practices (Taylor, 1911) and other HR practices (Bell, 1956) which are in conflict with values like independent work, creativity, and joy for workers. Move the clock ahead from the 1950s to more recent times where worker stories of lack of meaning and interest are described in similar terms (Sheehy, 1995; Palmer, 2007; Goldman, 2009; Lawrence-Lightfoot, 2009). The new generation of midlife adults is looking for new ways to navigate their own meaning and purpose in their lives (Corbett, 2006). In fact, Freedman (2011) suggests finding meaning in one's life becomes the whole reason for the rest of one's life.

Several researchers have agreed that ultimately we seek experiences to help us feel like what we do matters and it is an integrated part of our lives (Van Manen, 1990; Frankl, 1984; Evans & Bartolome 1981.). They suggest that when people enjoy their work they place a meaning, significance, and commitment on their work, and as a result the experience is far more enjoyable. Other researchers have gone further to suggest that life is meaning making itself of which freedom is a key to meaningful work (Csikszentmihalyi, 1990). The workers, who feel that their work is within the realm of choice as for instance they have the opportunity to choose tasks, the sequence, and pace of work, are likely to see their work as meaningful. Taken further, careers become a symbolic vehicle of self-representation and attempted self-perception (Ochberg, 1987). Once work is at this stage, a person is less likely to raise questions around if this is worth doing (Evans & Bartolome, 1981).

Despite the suggestion that meaningful work is important, the research tendency has been to focus on self-esteem, motivation, and so on (Deci, 1975; Herzberg, 1966). In fact, because of the greater focus on areas such as motivation, that has precluded more research on meaning and, as a result, motivation has become a surrogate for meaning (Sievers, 1986).

Enjoyment of Work

What are the factors that cause some people to enjoy their work and others simply to accept what they do? It was argued that scientific management principles from the turn of the century and even recent human resource techniques which are focused on efficiency and short-term results are in conflict with values that consider dignity, creativity, and joy in the workplace (Bell, 1956). HR practices which carry out performance appraisals rarely ask managers to be concerned about enjoyment and values for their workers as they do about competence (Evans & Bartolome, 1981). Managers tend to reinforce these HR policies by focusing in a person's capacity to do a job. For some people, rarely, the attention is paid to whether a person will enjoy and/or be proud of what he or she does (Evans & Bartolome, 1981). Only through deep reflection where the individual who asks, "Is this job worth doing and will I enjoy it?" versus the inexperienced person who simply asks, "Can I do it?" Many HR measurements of people's success do not recognize positive enjoyment of one's job as a company might measure production or a health professional might measure calorie intake. Some organizations are simply focused on production and behavior control (Csikszentmihalyi, 1975). Would people have more opportunities for enjoyment on the job if measurements were implemented to determine how much of a person's skills were actually utilized on a given job and how much flow could be expected? Could this assist HR in at least determining how much boredom could be expected and hence take different action rather than to simply increase the level of external rewards?

While enjoyment is often determined by the subjective experience of the individual, most jobs would not be done unless people were paid (Csikszentmihalyi, 1975). This could be a powerful incentive factor. The Chinese philosopher Chuang Tzu in 2000 AD believed that one can enrich the environment through focus and attention as opportunities are presented (Palmer, 2007). When employees start to enjoy their work and determine their own measure of success, this may take a huge dose of courage and conviction, especially for those HR programs which pay little attention to inner measures of success.

Herzberg (1966) suggests, in his work satisfaction theory, that many issues in the workplace are "dissatisfiers" if unpleasant but "satisfiers" if acceptable. It has also been suggested that people by nature love to hate their jobs and only hope that greater efforts will lead to more satisfaction (Halberstam, 2000; Csikszentmehalyi, 1988). Many workers fall into the trap of accepting the normal routine of work and demands of the job and start to lose a sense of control (Langer, 1997). While these same workers object to being treated as machines, they continue to experience work as largely dehumanizing (Terkel, 1975).

As was said earlier, some organizations focus on productivity, pay, and efficiency which continue to conflict with deep self-reflection. Unfortunately, for many workers work is simply a means to a larger end of providing a paycheck (Csikszentmihalyi, 1975). This leaves little time for self-reflection. Some people accept their work without allowing their dreams to intrude upon reality (Robin, 1998). Still, work impacts family and personal life and for some the size of the paycheck still determines how one feels about oneself and one's responsibilities. Thus, the relationship between work and career is a subjective experience which is influenced both by the environment as well as how one decides to direct one's life.

Choice and Calling

The Buddha said, "Work out your own salvation – do not depend on others" (Garfinkel, 2006, p. 22). This seems an appropriate way to start the discussion on vocation. Choosing one's vocation can be driven by many factors such as motivational maturity (Halberstam, 2000) and being open to one's experience and as a result being willing to make changes in one's work (Rodgers, 1961).

People tend to feel best when what they do is voluntary. They feel worst when what they do is obligatory. Without a consistent set of goals, it is difficult to develop a coherent self (Csikszentmihalyi, 1997). Others popular writers such as Sinetar (1987) and James (1955) suggested that you get more of what you focus on, and creating personal goals when making vocational choices could also raise self-esteem and provide momentum.

Another approach that may be helpful as suggested by Langer (1997) and Frankl (1984) is looking at prior choices of vocational path and to be open to other opportunities the second time. Super (1953) has suggested that choosing one's occupation is also an attempt to implement a self-concept and a vocational self-concept. To choose or follow one's occupation requires some definition of calling as a concept. Early, German-speaking Protestants described this as a *beruf* or calling. The idea was that it is not the type of work that matters as much as the pull it has on one's life.

With vocation, a person and the work he or she does are united. For example, a person could not change his or her work without change in being (Cochran, 1990). I have first-hand experience with this having left the corporate world of senior management to teach, write, and speak. Going back to doing the old management work would take a change in being and would be very difficult.

There are traditional ideas centered on understanding that for each of us there is a work for which we are naturally suited and gifted – a life's work (Boldt, 1996). John Stuart Mill was so inspired by his father's friend that he decided that the objective of his life was to reform the world (Cochran, 1990). Others have said that the highest calling requires following one's innermost soul (James, 1955; Moore, 1992). Several popular writers have written that some people may go through life luke-warm about what they are doing and yet their jobs remain too small for their spirits (Terkel, 1975; Toms & Toms, 1998).

Still, calling is the work one chooses to do (Halberstam, 2000). This comes despite the time it might take for many to finally break out of the pattern of incompletion in their vocational lives (Cochran, 1990).

This search is a responsibility to answer for one's life and not settle for an abstract meaning for one's work (Frankl, 1984). Some have called this a time to claim one's place at the fire to put focus on what we value most (Leider & Shapiro, 2004). At the same time, it remains that possibly it is just as important to perceive why one does a specific vocation in the first place. It starts with an examination and re-assessment of what one has done, is doing, and might do in the future.

The Criteria for Loving Work

Indian thinker Krishnamurti (1987) believed that there are many people who want to be famous because they don't love what they do. He believed that our present success is rotten because it teaches us to love success and not what we are doing. Results become more important than action. Loving what one does must include meaning otherwise it is difficult to distinguish a person with a vocation in life from someone who just likes his or her job (Cochran, 1990). A meaningful life seems necessary but not sufficient for happiness in one's vocation. The reverse is less possible. Few people manage to be happy if their lives are pointless and empty (Baumeister, 1991). It may be possible to retire from jobs but not from our individual calling (Leider & Shapiro, 2004).

In specific studies, it was observed that many people did activities simply for the sake of doing that activity without expecting any rewards for doing so (Csikszentmihalyi, 1975). It was simply their love of their work which drove them. The research seems to indicate that the first thing that one must do in getting started is to be open to re-examining one's work and the direction it is taking.

Making the Choice for Work

A Japanese proverb says that vision without an action is a daydream and an action without vision is a nightmare (Halberstam, 2000). Spiritual Indian leader Mohandas Gandhi believed that you must be the change that you want to see in the world (Carter, 1995). Other popular writers and researchers have suggested that the vision is important but taking action to move towards the dream is equally important (Toms & Toms, 1998; Cochran, 1990). They suggested that industry in many cases approaches the activity of work as a battle vs. as a playground. Within this battle, this could lead to people having difficulty within the context of a company in finding meaning in their work. This could be a result of the conflict between making money at all costs and finding joy in one's work.

Discovering what one loves to do can sometimes be a result of trying to solve a set of life problems which a person wishes to solve above everything else (Csikszentmihalyi, 1997). This can occur along with re-examination of what one has done, is currently doing, and wishes to do in the future. In fact, the regularity with which a person's later vocation is directly opposite of an initial one makes it difficult to understand why it had been neglected for so long (Ansbacher & Ansbacher, 1956). The Tibetians had a belief around this which said if you wanted to know your future, you should look at what you were doing in the present (Toms &

Toms, 1998). Sinetar (1987) suggested that one must search internally to reason and provide the necessary inspiration and courage and determination to seek out what one loves to do. When this occurs, work and play can be indivisible and work can be as enjoyable as leisure (Csikszentmihalyi, 1997).

For some people, following their love in vocation could be driven by the idea of generativity and concern for guiding the next generation (Erikson, 1986). Some people, in fact, in discovering the work they love to do feel like they have a need to make a difference (Sheehy, 1995). Still, it could remain important for people to know what they want from life; if they are not in touch with their passions neither do they take time for re-examination which ultimately could dictate their vocational choices.

Commitment to Work and Vocation

Sinetar (1987) said that an actualizing person is intrinsically involved with his or her work and uses it to understand the world around. Committing to the doing one's vocation is a crucial step towards evaluating one's progress, since it is our own appraisal which counts in the end (Halberstam, 2000). Some researchers have suggested that work is never finished for those with a vocation; neither can one rest in a vocation (Adler, 1964; Cochran, 1990). This contrasts with the widely popular theory of late stage career development of Super, (1953) where he describes a phasing down of career related activities as preparation for retirement. This notion of retirement is consistent with the society view over the past 50 years which prepares those for retirement with the gold watch, the 401K plan, and the retirement party (Freedman, 2011).

While in today's economic environment, people are forced to work longer there is still the expectation that instead they should retire and move aside for the younger workers. Can the experience of flow enhance one's commitment to his or her vocation? Flow theory suggests that flow occurs when a person faces a clear set of goals that require appropriate responses (Csikszentmihalyi, 1997). For example, flow theory suggests that matching high skills and low challenges causes one to become bored and anxious while matching low skills and low challenges can cause apathy. Matching high challenges and high skills is the way when one tends to lose oneself in the task and thus one's commitment can increase. When flow arises in actions taken toward a goal it can also increase commitment (Cochran, 1990). This begs the question about what should be in place to allow one to fully follow the vocation.

Being open to Experience and Knowing One's Self

Several researchers and a few popular writers have suggested that being open to one's experience and knowing one's self deeply can open the possibilities for vocation (Sinetar, 1987; Rodgers, 1961; Meneuhin, 1978; and Cochran, 1990). A 14th century author said "Swink and sweat in all that thou canst and mayst, for to get thee a true knowing and a feeling of thyself as thou art; and then I trow that soon after that thou shalt have true knowing and a feeling of God as He is" (Underhill, 2003, p.29). Translated this means one must try and experience different activities to get a true sense of what one enjoys. Being open to experience and asking oneself, "Have I created something which is satisfying to me and which truly expresses me?" can increase one's momentum towards vocation (Rodgers, 1961). This requires an inner locus of focus to both redirect attention and increase of one's self-efficacy (Bandura, 1980; Csikszentmihalyi, 1997). The need for re-examination, especially in midlife is an internal process which is inner directed. The results of this study will focus on these inner directed experiences which people in midlife have had while moving forward as a result of re-examination of their work related lives.

When work is inner directed, vocation can become something one can spend one's life doing (Scott & Jaffe, 2004). Many people in the quest for external yardsticks of success fail to look inward. This can be costly by continuing to do things which lack meaning and having an ongoing wish to be someone else (Norton, 1976). Other writers have suggested that when the meaning in life is broken, the quality of that life is diminished (Toms & Toms 1998; Bateson, 1972). When one's work is based on what is inside rather than outside, then whatever one has is sufficient. Many pursue their work for external reasons and in the end leave their lives to chance whether they will ever have enough. As one philosopher said, if you follow your bliss, you will have your bliss whether you have money or not. If you follow the money, you may lose money and then you don't even have that (Campbell, 1968). As Campbell suggests, pursuing money vs. doing something deeper leaves one empty inside in midlife.

Inner directed work takes an examination of one's life and representation of life (McAdams, Josselson, & Lieblich, 2006). The use of metaphor as a primary vehicle for holistic construction can help in guiding one towards internal work. For example, a person who views work as a war zone vs. a person who views work as a playground will each have a very different experience of work.

It is possible that the way in which one views one's work, for example, as a war versus an adventure may influence one's experience along the way (Pepper, 1942). In other words, there is a difference between how one can feel when having just a job and another one having a vocation. The use of story in understanding various critical life experiences such as significant people, events, highs and lows, and unresolved issues can help to create an inner story for one to rationalize and to find a path to follow (McAdams, Josselson, & Lieblich, 2006). As we live out our lives in story, this requires a continual alertness for distinctions which matter (Cochran, 1990). Story making helps self-realization by interpreting events in one's life (Jung, 1957).

Creating one's vision or story can provide the feeling that following one's interest area or vocational path was the right thing to do and everything would work out overtime (Rodgers, 1961). Real confidence comes from knowing and accepting oneself and one's vision while working to provide a climate in which external evaluations are absent (Bardwick, 1986; Rodgers, 1961). Proust said, "The voyage of discovery lies not in finding new landscapes but in having new eyes" (Toms & Toms, 1998, p. 28). This requires one to be resourceful and determined with one's vision to perform independent thinking about where one is going, as described by Sinetar (1987). Asking one's self about the meaning of the life without self-evaluators and negative internal feedback can provide the path towards deeply knowing one's self (Toms and Toms, 1998). Jung said, "My life is what I have done and my works can be regarded as a station along my life's way" (Jaffe, 1984, p.25). This helps to define vocation.

Following a vocational path which feels meaningful and more aligned with one's abilities and interests is difficult as it leads one into unknown territory. However, it may be easy because it leads you toward doing what you love. For example, the pure joy of doing activities in one's work that are full of meaning and purpose can help to defeat the negative emotions which can be encountered during changes in one's work. It starts with the love of what you do and who you are. It is as William James (1955) said, you have to act as if what you do makes a difference.

Fulfillment and Meaning in Midlife

Some popular writers have concluded that people get stuck in their routines and find it difficult to practice spontaneity (Levoy, 1997; Toms & Toms 1998). When a realization comes that new choices might make one's life uncomfortable during the transition could make it difficult to follow one's deeply felt aspirations. Is it easier to live in a world of "maybes where we only look at others for their views? Some people may consistently struggle with conflict, fear, and the "what if" syndrome. What exists when conflict ends? According to Steinem (2006), the biggest problem of our society is being youth oriented along with pressure to retire and live a life of dependency after 60.

As the popular literature suggests, conflict can be a waste of energy and wears out a person psychologically when this thinking is based on worry, projection, or fear (Krishnamurti, 1987). Some people may avoid the anxiety of saying yes to new choices. In the interim, this approach can steal decades from one's life. This occurs when people don't re-examine what they have done, are doing, or want to do with their working life. In this case they end up erecting an emotional barrier between themselves and their work. In many cases, there is a tendency to separate work and life. As early as c.50 it was said by Epictetus that first, one has to make clear to oneself what to do and then do what one has to do (Matheson, 1916).

Although often people become programmed for failure or limited success and in response, set lower goals. By doing this, they move away from what they want. This leads to later burnout (Scott & Jaffe, 2004). Only by being self-directed, can we possibly avoid these pitfalls. Our life always expresses the result of our dominant thoughts. The things we believe, expect, and tell ourselves generally determine what we accomplish (Swenson, 2000). In many cultures, any impulse to step outside one's cautious, predictable life was a sign of trouble. This followed a belief that change is impulsive, foolish, and dangerous. It is in contrast to human nature which is a movement towards growth and health or actualization of human potential as described by popular mid-life writer Leshan (1973). It is possible that once we are confronted with the need to change for further growth, we are conditioned to avoid doing what is required. Many of us took on current work roles either by chance or because other people directed us into work based on their expectations. As a result, some people may be afraid to quit, and we say, *"It can't be done"* before we have the evidence (Leshan, 1973). This pessimism can take off all energy required to follow a vocational path in midlife (Toms & Toms, 1998).

Many authors suggested that work begins when one does not like what one is doing, and this suffering is the start to finding some greater meaning in one's work (Frankl, 1984; Campbell, 1968). Still, some people often end up trading their authenticity for what we perceive as survival, terrified to swap security for what we truly desire (Levoy, 1997). As a result, the corrosive effects of avoidance also exact their toll on our emotional and physical lives.

Breaking through the Barriers of New Growth in Midlife

Becker (1971) has stated that our self-esteem depends on our inner news-reel. Perhaps, it can be helpful to ask oneself specifically about one's purpose while reviewing one's autobiography as a source of self-examination for continual renewal (Fromm, 1994).

What is your inner newsreel saying right now? How do you feel about that?

While there are many reasons why people put off discovering and following a vocational path in midlife there also may be reasons why one should re-examine this critical element of one's life. Perhaps, we should start with an ancient view of Dante on what is the mid-life journey: "In the middle of the journey of our life, I came to myself in a dark wood, for the straight way was lost. Ah, how hard it is to say what that wood was, so savage and harsh and strong that the thought of it renews my fear. It is so bitter that death is little more so!" (Alighieri, 1996, p. 23).

The research suggests that many people indeed do not have the experience of loving what they do in their vocational life. It is not easy to find the vocational path in midlife without being swallowed up by a slave morality (May, 1973) or being dehumanized which prevents inner searching (Marx, 1963). So many people judge the value of their actions not by the action itself but how the action will be accepted. In midlife, this fear of acceptance, lack of self-evaluation, and inner direction does not support the challenges one will face during this period of life. This is a period of disenchantment and realization that we have already lived more years than the number that lie ahead (Raines, 1994).

It takes a realization that new actions may now be necessary to overcome this period of disenchantment with regards to one's vocation if one is uncomfortable. It comes at a time when protecting one's self-esteem is high and taking career risks can seem like the unsafe thing to do (Becker, 1973; Raines, 1994). Jung may have said it best when he remarked, "Wholly unprepared, they embark upon the second half of life when we take the step into the afternoon of life; worse still we take this step with the false assumption that our truths and ideals will serve as before" (Welch, 1982, p. 95).

Despite this, there are those individuals who seek harmonious participation with their environment by taking control of their vocational lives (Csikszentmihalyi, 1975) and others who leave no time for introspection or contemplation of the meaning in their lives (Brehony, 1996). Those individuals who do seek this deeper meaning find tension between what they have already accomplished and what they want to achieve (Frankl, 1984). Those who ignore their passions dam up energies and cut themselves off from finding new callings and rather than demonstrate their passion wait for their passions to show up (Moore, 1992). The research suggests that vocational happiness occurs when people line up their goals and passions with something which is important to them (Csikszentmihalyi, 1997). This requires an authentic curiosity about how one is using energy (Borysenko, 2011).

Additionally, the more consciousness of one's self one has, the more spontaneous and creative one can be. Awareness comes in rare moments. It is as if a person stands on top of a mountain peak and views his or her life from a new and wide perspective (May, 1973). This self-consciousness could start the process in midlife to experience a better alignment of one's work- related life.

Little research has been done to describe what the actual experience is like for people who do re-align and follow their abilities along with their work-related passions in midlife. In my research I wanted to understand how these lives are affected so as to provide guideposts for others seeking similar change.

The new era of Retirement and Redefinition

The research suggests that there is a need to shift views of retirement in midlife and beyond to a new set of terms. Bateson (2010) described "Adulthood II" as the primary child-rearing and career-building period. After this period of life follows a time of reflection and movement toward what a person would rather do, which usually is different from what he or she was doing before. There was once a well-known truism suggesting that in life there are no second acts (Chope, 2011). This way of thinking is changing now as midlife adults pursue new activities after reflection.

In many ways, the idea of retirement is a new idea in American history as in the past people worked until they dropped (Freedman, 2011). While most have become familiar with the mid-life crisis as a point in life for re-examination, it's the time for punctuation, and a fresh new start (Bateson, 2010).

Corbett (2006) refers to the midlife period of life as the "anti-retirement" or the "portfolio life." This portfolio life will be filled with a variety of activities and pursuits focused around one's core interests. These core interests should be a core focus in midlife (Tracey, 2007). Thus, a large part of our society will be thinking deeply about existential questions, happiness and meaning in this stage of life. Freedman (2011) has called this period of life "an encore career," searching for the freedom to work vs. saving for retirement. This group will be a growing group of people who have rejected retirement in exchange for pursuing work as a destination. How do you feel about the word retirement?

My Own Values and Beliefs

In the United States, people have many opportunities to align their interests and abilities in midlife. At the same time, they may be held back because of many fears. Some may have fear of failing. Others, fear of success. All this possibly contributes to keeping people from doing more of what they love in their vocational life. Many people put off their dreams, their desires for the time when they retire. Unfortunately, upon retirement, they might find themselves having difficultly finally getting started at this stage of their life to finally do what they love. In many cases, illness, aging, fears, and just lack of wanting to take risks might contribute to making it difficult to start new vocational change.

I believe that many people have the ability in midlife to create a greater sense of purpose about their life while further defining what is most important. I believe that people in midlife have the ability to create new perspective, possibilities while shedding old work-related masks and attitudes, which are no longer useful. I think in midlife, it is possible to further define what one is passionate about which can lead to greater energy and a greater sense of fulfillment and meaning about one's life each and every day. I also believe that there are significant challenges to deal with in midlife when contemplating change in one's work.

Many people in midlife have too many material responsibilities. As a result, there must be a sacrifice to making a major change in midlife to pursue one's passion with intent on making a living. Personal change can lead to greater happiness, sense of place in the world, and overall feeling that one's life means something. This may or may not be true for many people. And hopefully my research will give some answers for those who are searching for them.

Midlife can be a time for anxiety and turmoil. Many people don't reflect on their life outside their traditional work environment on what they would do if they had unlimited flexibility and opportunity. Some people during this time of life confront mortality for the first time. This can lead to transition.

As the research has indicated, this transition can feel like a crisis. Some adults at this point re-assess whether their work is a proper fit. Some do not feel contented given they are not driven by negative thoughts and emotions. Additionally, alienation can occur when a person feels losing the ability to direct the part of life that he or she has invested in work.

Career theory-influenced approaches for looking at job fit, skill evaluation, and personality assessment. Although, traditional counseling has tended to neglect meaning and choice in favor of more generally accepted developmental approaches. As a result, when workers lose meaning, they do not live up to their capacity and experiments of organizational motivational programs.

Several researchers have suggested that at work we should experience activities which help us to feel like what we do matters. However, managers and HR programs tend to reinforce HR policies by focusing on a person's capacity to do a job vs. if he or she will enjoy doing it. James (1955) suggested that reaching one's highest calling requires following one's innermost soul. Further on, being open to experience and knowing one's self deeply can open possibilities for vocation (Rodgers, 1961; Meneuhin, 1978; Fromm, 1994). Also, the research has shown that midlife can be the time for disenchantment and realization that the time left is shorter than the time lived and the time when protecting one's self-esteem is key and risks seem unwise (Becker, 1971).

From the research reviewed, it is important to study those in midlife who took control of their environment. This will help others to understand the experience and results of vocational re-alignment in midlife. My research was an attempt to extend the work of other researchers to go deeper into the actual experience of those people who discovered and transitioned their work in midlife to work which was both a better alignment of their passions, abilities, and interests and which provided more meaning.

Learning Through Others and Their Stories

I believe that we can learn from others who have been where we want to go.

I was interested in finding out what challenges these individuals faced and how their lives changed as a result of following their work-related passions. The literature shows that much of the accepted counseling and traditional career development methods neglect the inner meanings of vocation and choice for people in midlife. It is critical to better align a person's passions and self-interests and abilities. The descriptions of these experiences enhanced the knowledge and understanding of what mid-life adults went through while going through transition. This new knowledge and awareness could provide additional frames of reference to assist the growing population of mid-life adults who are going through the vocational transitions. In my research, I wanted to know what was the described experience of mid-life adults who changed their vocational path to work which has more meaning for them.

In the next section, you will read a summary of the analysis of the interviews with my participants. If you want to read more details of each participant's transition please see The Interviews section at the back of the book.

As you read through this next section, make some notes about your own thoughts and experiences. I will have some exercises for you to do after each section!

The Participants

(All names used as pseudonyms)

Julie, a 45-year-old White middle-class female, lives in the Pacific Northwest, and transitioned from working for large organizations in human resources for 20 years to her new work as a non-profit executive in the health industry.

Sam, a 55-year-old White middle-class male, lives in Northern California, and spent a long career working in sales roles in large organizations before getting laid off. Now he works as a college instructor.

Janet, a 55-year-old White middle-class female, lives in the Midwest, and spent many years in an administrative job after raising her children. Today, she describes her work as the owner of her own marketing and writing Internet business.

Juan, a 46-year-old, Hispanic middle-class male, lives in Northern California, and spent many years as a manager in the banking system on the East Coast before getting laid off. Now he is an entrepreneur.

Riya, a 43-year-old Indian middle-class female, lives in Northern California, and spent many years in the High Tech industry as a PhD engineer and then decided to leave. Today, she describes her work as a technical consultant and a teacher in the healing arts, teaching physics to healers.

Kyle, a 50-year-old White middle-class male, lives in the Southwest, and spent many years in sales before his divorce led him to a new work. He owns a real estate investment company now.

Charlie, a 55-year-old White middle-class male, lives in the Southwest, and after many years working as a cosmetic dentist quit after his father died. Today, he works as a writer, healer, teacher and speaker.

Ann, a 55-year-old White middle class female, lives in the Pacific Northwest, and spent many years as a hairdresser and stay-at-home mom. Today, she works as an advisor helping people to make money from home, and she runs her own Internet business.

I am deeply grateful to these participants for allowing me to interview them in order to understand their transitions from work which held little meaning to work which is more fulfilling and a better alignment to their abilities and interests in their lives.

The Experience of the "Treadmill" of Life and Work

The participants described their life situations and their previous work environments in different ways which as a result of analysis emerged in three subthemes.

Work did not bring satisfaction.

Most participants described that they had long-term careers in a variety of fields such as sales, human resources, banking, administration, technology, medicine, and beauty care. Despite the difference in the types of work they were doing, the participants were not satisfied with their work.

> Uh, highly stressful, um, mainly a lot of anxiety, um, although – [Laughs] It was uh, my life was uh, very stressful, a lot of anxiety, um, um, money worries, we, we always had enough money. We always made good money but for some reason, I still harbored a lot of internal fear because uh, it just wasn't, I just didn't feel stable. (Kyle)

> Not only was I a little bit bored, but I had this, um – a depression coming on because my soul was not being fulfilled. (Riya)

The participants experienced a lot of work anxiety that didn't seem that much different for the four men and four women I interviewed. They experienced a feeling of angst about their work, tiredness from the routine, wanting something more, but not being sure what. As participants spoke about their past, they showed strong emotions as they described their current state at the time. They wanted their work to give them more satisfaction. They wanted to see a stronger connection to where their work was leading them.

> I was living with a lot of anxiety — and, um, trying to make things right, um, but very bored. Um, uh, feeling a little bit, um, guilty. I wouldn't say guilty, but, uh, not having a very strong image — of myself. Not – not really, um, uh, seeing myself as someone with, um, consistency, but integrity. Um, and I think a little insecure.

> It was like that. That was, um, and morbid. I think I didn't have – I didn't have observations for the future. (Juan)

> Working at a regular J-O-B, it was, um, confining. I felt trapped. I didn't like somebody else telling me when I can eat and when I can't eat.

> And when I can do this or that. So, um, I found it very confining.

> Uh, yeah, well, I think – anxiety I think would be a good, uh, summary. (Riya)

The participants were looking for something although they were not sure what that would free them from this feeling of unease. All connected their unease to their work and they wanted to find a way out to something else although they had not defined it as yet. As they talked more, I discovered this feeling of being disconnected from their work also led to feeling disconnected with others.

Feeling disconnected with others.

Some participants felt alone, some disconnected with others. Juan, who was working at the bank as a manager, described himself as feeling like an alien on a different planet. Riya, who was working in the high tech industry after putting in long hours and long days, felt like she no longer fit.

> Well, um, I was, you know, the moment that I left the car to walk into the office, I could feel the anxiety and my – my breathing was… was different. I was breathing differently. Um, and the experience of walking into an office was the same experience of walking to another planet. Uh, in a sense that people were aliens. I didn't have that sense of – of relatedness with people. (Juan)

> I thought I had put all this effort into adding creativity into my work and being – doing a big contribution that I thought was creative, a creative way to contribute just – and I had tried to work with, um, you know, the organizational development people and the human resources people and all that to make –the work

life better and, uh, ranking and rating came along, and I was – so it looked like I was gonna be demoted.

And that seemed – it just seemed like I didn't fit the situation, and I didn't wanna play anymore. (Riya)

Others, like Julie didn't feel appreciated or valued like a high priced cog in the wheel. She found herself thinking deeper about what she would rather do.

Oh, my goodness. Um – Typical day would've started at 6:00 a.m. with East Coast or international conference calls. Sometimes they were in the middle of the night because I was doing international work. Um, often travel. I traveled about 70 to 80 percent of the time. Um, and nonstop meetings, nonstop pressure, nonstop firefighting. Um, a lot of emotion because I was in HR, obviously. A lot of people issues that, that are pretty draining.

Um, I'm an introvert by nature and I didn't realize at the time how draining that really was for me. This led me to feeling disconnected from what I wanted and the organization.

Um, I was leading a large team. They were scattered all over, so I never really had that, um, never really had a feeling of having it all together because there was just so much going on and so quickly. I never felt like I could be completely successful. It was just kind of spiraling, um, it was so much all the time.

And often working, you know, weekends. And the, the workday never really ended. You could, you know, you could never really call it done. (Julie)

This described experience from Julie was consistent among the participants that the cycle of work that each was involved in was becoming overwhelming and not sustainable. Although, most participants were doing well by society standards, they wanted something deeper, more fulfilling in their work.

There were, however, differences between participants. Janet, a stay at home mom, for many years felt it was natural to feel disconnected from others in her role. In her case, it was a natural evolution to try something new when her kids were grown and her husband's health improved. This was very different from Charlie who suddenly didn't feel connected any longer to his field of dentistry and patients and coworkers. So while I observed that the experience was slightly different for each participant, this feeling of disconnect created strong emotions towards wanting to change. The participants were consistent and clear that their work at the time carried little meaning for them.

Work was endless and carried little meaning.

The participants described consistently that they were working hard for firms in never ending cycles of long hours and few rewards. A few participants discussed feeling little creativity with no time for more interesting work with substance. At the same time, it was common for most participants that they were just working to pay the bills and make ends meet; they expended lots of activity but experienced little personal value. Many described their work lives as fearful, hectic, and working long hours. Ann summed this up best.

> Well, I had been working like 90 hours a week because of our situation because of, you know, just trying to keep up with – you know, keep our house up, the medical expenses and things like that. So I was really worn out. (Janet)

Many participants had this feeling of being caught in a never ending wheel of work. Janet described this feeling as follows:

> You wake up at 6:00. You go to work early in order to be at work at 8:00 or 8:30 and, um, you know, and you work all day. Um,

you go – I went to the gym at – After work. And then I came home, I had a couple of hours of, uh, to eat and to, um, just, you know, catch up on stuff, and then I would go to bed and I would repeat it. Day after day after day after day. A rat in a maze. (Janet)

This illustrates how the participants experienced their work at the time. Although they each had very different backgrounds, their described experiences with their work were similar; endless cycles of work without meaning or purpose. Still their work lives carried on in the same fashion until an event occurred to move them to action.

Internal and External Triggers Pushed the Need for Change

The participants described the different life events which influenced their decision towards making major change in their life and work.

Divorce, layoff, death of a relative.

It was interesting to learn that some participants had an external trigger event that occurred which led to the need for change. Charlie saw his father die, Juan was laid off, Sam suffered an injury, Kyle went through a divorce. This led them to search for new options.

It was something very specific in a very specific time and place.

My father had passed away, and I was headed east on Speedway Boulevard in Tucson; my father had passed away a couple of weeks earlier, and I was like, "Wow," all of a sudden in this one moment I thought, "Man, I'm gonna die too." And in that very moment, I – I said, "I've got to do something about my life," and I made a commitment to myself to take six months off to travel and take pictures, which is what I was most passionate about. And then – then between the time that I – that I – I said I was leaving November 1st. It was like, "I'm going no matter what." (Charlie)

For Kyle, his divorce was a shock and a trigger event that caused him, unlike the rest, not to move quickly into a new direction but to initially freeze not knowing what to do next!

Real estate was something I was always interested in. It's funny because when I was 20 years old, my mom was a real estate agent. I bought my first property. And, at that point at the table, I remember I didn't know anything. I was a 20-year-old kid sitting around the table with lawyers and real estate agents and, and it was so exciting to me that I never did it again for 30 years [laughs] or 25 years. It was so exciting I'm like I walked out of that office after I signed all these paperwork which I didn't know

– you know, it's just, I was basically a teenager.

And I bought a house. My mom had helped me buy this house and uh, I was working of course but, but uh, I always had that at the back of my head like that was really cool when I did that, you know? And for – and I always thought about it. Then, uh, I watched the show called Flip This House…Uh, you know, I got handed the divorce papers out of the blue and, and that was it. That was the straw. Does that make sense? (Kyle)

The one thing I noticed was that the men seemed to be affected more by the external trigger events in their lives compared to the women. This may relate to gender differences and the tendency for men to not make major moves until they have no choice but to change.

Sudden realization of the need to change.

The women seemed more confident and clear about their situations and what they should do after a sudden realization that they need to do their change. For example, Julie and Riya had made risky decisions to quit after a sudden realization that came to them.

Without any breathing room or recovery space. Um, and that, you know, financially I was in a place, you know, after having given 20 years in corporate America, that I could take some risks. Um, I was questioning, honestly, whether I needed to get out of HR, whether I needed to get out of corporate America, or whether I needed to get out of both and just kind of start fresh. And it was a whole, like, you know, rethinking my identity because I'm an HR gal. Um, so I did. I, I literally walked away. I gave notice, um, you know, on the heels of a potentially very large promotion and, um, went to work for the – I just completely changed. (Julie)

Decisions and risks were made given each person's economic situation which influenced the next steps they took. Riya suffered a small injury rushing to work which for her was a wakeup call.

I just started reading, and it sparked something in me. And I thought that sounded really appealing, and I just – Um, I wanted to have the freedom to do what I wanted and do something that I loved instead of, uh, being pigeonholed into, you know, "You don't have a degree, you don't have this and that, this and that, so you can only do this and you can only make this much." (Riya)

Ann, whose husband was ill for many years, decided to seek

entrepreneurial activities only after his recovery. In Ann's case, after years of administrative jobs, she decided to start an Internet business after her internal search for self-discovery. So from participants I understood that although all of them wanted to change, it was not until an external or internal trigger event occurred that they decided to move towards change.

Internal push for change.

It was clear from the interviews that all participants wanted something more out of their work lives. For Sam, Ann, Riya and Julie the time was moving too fast as they described, and they felt an internal push to do something very different from what they were doing. For Sam, Juan and Kyle, there was much unease about what to do next.

> I was on a 100 percent commission so, I worked to early afternoon on your early days and then I would get off for that afternoon during the weekday and then on the later days, I would be up a little – I would go in say at 2:00 in the afternoon, work till 10:00 at night. I would have a day off during the week and, then you'd work the weekend I mean the weekends you worked every single weekend. I just didn't know what to do next. (Kyle)

All participants described this time of their lives as a realization that doing nothing at this point was not an option. Participants expressed these feelings in different ways but all did not feel connected to their work.

One morning, I had to be on an early morning meeting. But I had to get my car serviced, and I — you know, juggling a bunch of things, so I had this early appointment at the – at the service center, and I went up there and dropped off the car and ran to catch a cab just so I could get back home to get on the morning meeting, and I whacked myself in the head in the third eye. [Giggles]. And it – and it started bleeding, and so that was a wake-up call, like try – you know, was it really worth all that just to get on to a silly meeting. (Riya)

It's definitely one of those things where I, I just felt that I was gonna get back on the treadmill one more time, and I couldn't do it anymore, and I wanted to live a more authentic life, enjoying what am I doing and not just working to make ends meet. And even that was not something that was reliable. I'm being told, "Doing a great job, but you're making too much money." Giving then with – Commission cuts, having jobs I had outsourced offshore, downsized, reengineered regardless of my performance. And of course if the company was having a tough time, I could get laid off for not making, making quota. And I had felt just the working was like looking for work all the time. You go in to –

Even except I was getting a commission check, you know? It just – And I'd been – Just couldn't, I just couldn't do that anymore. (Sam)

Uh, [laughs]. I think – I think was the – the humiliation. Um, four – four times I think being laid off. Um, I told myself, you know, I don't wanna be humiliated anymore. (Juan)

In listening to the participants it was clear that a combination of feeling empty and withdrawn from their work and external trigger events for some participants was enough to take the next step towards change and take time for reflection.

Time for Reflection, Self-Awareness, and Self-Care

As a result of analysis of the interviews, all participants after the internal or external triggers, took time to reflect deeply about their lives and their work and what they wanted. This reflection took many shapes.

Going through healing.

Several participants described the need to settle past wounds and or heal before fully moving forward in their transitions. The reasons were very different between each person. For example, Julie just needed to get away from what she described as the rat race which made her feel depressed.

Charlie needed to take off and travel. Kyle needed time to recover or repair after wounded relationships. As well, Juan and Sam needed to build self-confidence after their layoff.

> Uh, so, for ten years, I just struggled, uh, lost energy and was stagnant. Uh, and then through the traumatic divorce there was nothing left anymore, there was nowhere to go. Uh, so it was either do or die at that point. (Kyle)

> I think the greatest thing was just finding myself and replacing the idea of there's something wrong with me. (Juan)

> Um, I think that as I'm starting to write my bio lately is that I made this break with – with cultural reality. I took off and I left the United States, and I found out there's all these different ways to be and to do. (Charlie)

Riya took time to explore her spiritual side.

> So when I was exploring the "soul" part, the – you know, the – the – the creative work, *The Artist's Way*, I – I did yoga teacher training and started studying Shamanic practices, and so this was a, you know, continuation return to – to that. So I was – you – I wasn't employed full time, and I had time to finish this training in energy medicine and healing arts. (Riya)

With Ann and Janet, I didn't see the same pattern of needing to heal as they did not experience any traumatic situations. All participants though described this liminal state where some time was needed for self-care.

Needed to step back and reflect.

Each participant took time for reflection in their own way. For some like Riya and Sam, this meant trying out new roles in new areas. For others such as Julie, it meant taking time to be away.

> Uh, it was interesting. Once, I shed the label and, um, I took that year, kinda academic year, um, as this career adviser, um, it became really obvious that I was not going back to corporate America. Um, but I still loved HR. And, um, the dream job just landed in my lap. Truly, once, once I opened my eyes, um, within, within days this dream job landed in my lap, and I've never looked back.
>
> And I realize now in hindsight that that was really my own year of self-reflection. In my new role I was in a school to give advice to students, but really I was advising myself throughout that year. (Julie)

For Charlie, reflection meant action and adventure.

I gave myself space to allow for something greater than I had imagined, so instead of taking six months off, it ended up being – it ended up being indefinite, and I ended up doing a two and a half year adventure driving from Tucson all the way to the southern tip of South America. (Charlie)

I learned from the group that this need for self-reflection was a prerequisite to making any changes in their life. While the participants took different approaches the goal was the same, which was to find new directions for their work and life.

Exploring new opportunities.

The participants described that they took time to explore new opportunities. For them this was finding a new path, a new direction, and an opportunity to try out their creative sides. Juan enrolled in college to learn how to produce movies. Charlie was writing a book. Riya opened up a spiritual practice. All three discussed these projects with great passion describing that they felt free to finally try out some new ideas without perceived constraints. These, however, were not the final paths that these participants ended up doing.

I was extremely passionate about the book that I was writing. (Charlie)

Oh, I think, uh, it made a lot, uh, bigger difference. Yeah, because I get to communicate with people, you know, around the world and have had communications from people, you know, in over 100 countries. And, um, you know, it's – it's fun. (Ann)

Julie worked for one year as a career counselor.

Uh, it was interesting. Once, I shed the label and, um, I took that year, kinda academic year, um, as this career adviser, um, it became really obvious that I was not going back to corporate America. (Julie)

While the movement in the new direction was exciting and internally motivating it also led to the next stage and the challenges that the participants would encounter.

Change was Difficult

The participants described the challenges that each went through in their transitions and how they dealt with these challenges.

Unknown path.

For most of the participants, it was not clear what they would do next. Juan thought something creative like making movies would be fun. Charlie wanted to write books and travel and Riya wanted to do something in marketing. Ann was open to many possibilities but not clear. Sam wanted to teach. Julie wanted to do something in the community. She approached this unknown path with deep questions about what she might do next.

> Wow, what, could I be? What could I be if this label wasn't attached, you know, squarely to my forehead? Um, if I wasn't living behind this, you know, title? What, what are those other things I'm interested in and, and truly how do I want to spend the rest of my career? (Julie)

Riya wanted to pursue her spiritual side. Kyle always loved real estate but wasn't clear how he could turn that into making money. What the group had in common was the need and desire to do something which they enjoyed but in all cases except Ann and Julie, the immediate need to make money to live was also the main concern. Both Ann and Julie had working husbands at the time, which I believe presented a little more breathing space to try out new options with less money pressure.

Sam described the challenge of the unknown path he took shortly after being laid off and injured. His wife worked but after going through losing a house and bankruptcy the need to make sustainable money was an ongoing pressure.

And so the – And, uh, I went back to work at, uh, the temporary job, uh, writing marketing materials for a friend of mine's business who has an eBay auction house. So I was writing ad copy and, uh, as sort of a survival job. Trying to think what I'm going to do next. (Sam)

For some participants, this work and life transition also meant a change in relationships.

Loss of friends.

Juan described the experience of selling all his material goods and initially moving to Florida with his dog alone, no friends, and no clear idea what he would do next. He said after his move it was difficult to meet new friends until he was clear what he was doing. He wasn't sure how he would tell new friends who he was or what he was doing. Although the participants didn't specifically address this, it was interesting to note that during the time when they were in transition without a firm role or job title they had a hard time keeping in touch with their friends.

Uh, some went away as friends, and others, especially long-time friends, they just sort of watch in curiosity, and in – in a way, they know me – they've known me before I had any other career, so they just know that's Riya. She likes to explore. She does, you know – tons of people that know – knew me – my essential self. (Riya)

While Julie, Ann, and Sam had healthy relationships to support them during their transitions, Charlie, Janet, and Kyle took the path alone. Janet discussed that if she ever met someone to form a new relationship they would need to understand and support her lifestyle.

I don't really have friends. Unknowingly, at the time. But you know, significant relationships, I guess if I, you know, ever have one or, you know, like a significant man/woman relationship, I think it would really affect it because even if they work, you know, in a full-time job, um, it still – You know, I would accept that. That's what their calling is. But it would affect me because I'm, I just want to be accepted for having a different mindset. (Janet)

In some ways, I observed that not having a close support network during this challenging time of their life made their transition a longer process.

Trial and error.

All participants moved quickly to try out new roles which they were curious about. Julie tried student counseling for about a year. Juan enrolled in a film college for a few months before realizing that this was not practical for him. Janet developed a website to promote her marketing business. Sam started support groups for parents with children who had autism. Riya started her spiritual practice. Charlie drove to South America and Kyle started to sell cars to support himself during the transition from divorce. Ann, free of parenting responsibility, took on a new adventure.

> Well, um, when I decided to make the switch, I went to work for a marketing company, and they were, uh, launching in Australia. And so they asked for volunteers that wanted to go over to Australia to help launch the business over there. And so, you know, again, I was, you know, just really eager for a change and enthusiastic. And I – I knew, again, I needed to, you know – I sold my – my business. And so I – I needed to make a good income pretty quickly. So I offered to go. I said hey, this is a great opportunity. They offered to pay us – double our income if we met the president's challenge and were successful. (Ann)

What was consistent, however, for all participants was that their next move was only temporary. Each described a series of trial and error work related moves that would meet both their desire for work with more meaning and income that would be enough to support them.

I did yoga teacher training and started studying Shamanic practices, and so this was a, you know, continuation– I wasn't employed full time, and I had time to finish this training in energy
medicine and healing arts and continued and have continued as I
have the patent litigation because there's all this flexibility, and I
have a lot of – I give it a lot of respect and value. (Riya)

For many, this search for stable work and happiness didn't come
so easily.

I was on a 100 percent commission. So, a lot of, a lot of stagnant
time was, made up a lot of my day which, which made it even
worse because you just didn't know –I just didn't know where the
next check was coming pretty much. (Kyle)

While there were differences in the level of struggle which each
participant went through, all of them had to go through financial struggles.

Financial hurdles.

For many participants there were adjustments to be made in their financial situation. Charlie who initially lived off an inheritance and money
from selling his dental practice soon needed to make many adjustments.

It certainly got less and less, and I got to a point where I actually, um, I actually gave my house back to the bank, and so talk about a major, uh, turnaround, going from feeling like, you know, the bank took my house, and, um, and – and yet, an interesting little story. I was driving around, and ended up staying at – in a kind of house-sitting situation for a long time, and then I ended up moving in with my mom, which turned out to be a pretty good situation in the long run, but at one point in time, I had been playing with my nephew, and playing in the par, and I ran up this slide that we were playing on, and I ran into this pole, smacked myself right in the nose, and I – as a reflex, I chomped down, and my bottom teeth hit my top teeth, and I broke six teeth. It always makes people cringe when I tell them the story. And so I didn't have the money to get my teeth fixed, and I looked pretty gnarly, and I'm driving around in a fairly beat up car that's got dents on three out of four sides. I hadn't bought any new clothes in a couple of years, and I'm living at home with my mom. Can you say loser? (Charlie)

Making money was a constant worry throughout the transition and even after the new beginning for Janet and Sam.

Money – Financially, um, just worrying about chasing – You know, you're always chasing, um, to, to make what you need to live on. (Janet)Big thing. I'm, I'm teaching my immune sys – I, I mean my, uh, um, nervous system to calm down when the unexpected bill comes in or, um, an opportunity dries up. I, I'm always looking for the, looking for some new thing. Trying to build this, trying to build that. You know, keeping the working going on. Even if I'm, you know, booked 100 percent, you never know what's gonna come on down the pike, so always looking for those opportunities. (Sam)

Julie and Ann described similar situations when, with their working husbands, financial hurdles were minimal.

Julie: I know that I'll never go back to for-profit funding. Um, my heart is in this work. Even if it's not this organization, which I hope it is, but even if it's not, um, it – My heart is in the non-profit sector, and I see such a need for, um, talent. I see such a need for, you know, partnerships and have gifts that I can give here.

All participants, however, described their new beginning as needing some adjustments either emotional or financial. All said that eventually this new road led to feeling better about themselves. I learned that for most participants the joy of leaving the old job soon turned into its own series of challenges.

A New Beginning

Even though the participants described the financial and lifestyle adjustments that each had to go through while making change, at the same time they all described a new sense of self, more confidence, happiness and better relationships. As a result, the analysis emerged in subthemes as follows:

Better sense of self.

All participants described feeling better about themselves and what they were doing. They discussed feeling more content, happier, and calm about where they were now in life. They described that they felt excited about every day.

> Um, I feel more confident, more self-confident than I ever was before.

> Um, I feel more in control of my life because I am doing what I want to do. I can structure my business any way I want to do. I am the boss, nobody's micromanaging me, I can micromanage

myself if I want to. (Janet)

Nothing to defend. I feel more settled with myself. Like there is nothing to prove. I felt really good about myself and that has a big part, that's a big thing to do with it. Even if I set an alarm, I'm awake a little bit before it, naturally, um, and so I feel excited — about whatever's to come that day, or it's not excited anticipating a day that you solve some puzzles and have a little, you know, fun. (Riya)

Well, it's like — as I said before, right now in this moment in my life, I'm just as excited to get up in the morning and excited to go to bed because of what I'm gonna dream about. (Charlie)

So what I have today that I didn't have three years ago is that I have dreams, right, so I have plans, I have something that I wake up in the morning and my future gives my presence. (Juan)

I found from the interviews that the participants described that they felt more secure not in a financial sense but in their emotional state of mind. I noticed there was less anxiety as they spoke, more confidence and sense of direction for them. I found this led to better relationships.

Better relationships.

I was interested to find out how the participants' relationships changed as a result of their transitions. I wanted to understand both their closest relationships as well as casual friends. Some participants were more open about this. Janet and Juan were fairly closed about this but did say that they thought new people that they would meet today would find them happier, easier to be around.

> I have a better relationship with myself and I'm happier — with myself. And, um, I'm relating — I relate with people in a different way. Yeah, so, um, I'm happier as, and I'm — I'm happier in my relationships, too, so it's easier to make friends — easier to listen to people. (Janet)

Charlie described how his family relationships improved.

> Well, it's interesting, because right now, I'm — in the past year or two, I have sort of re- — I've gotten back into relationships with my family, my immediate family. Not my children family, but my mother and my siblings, and my sisters, uh, my sister, who is just a little bit older than me, is going through some health kind of related, mental health challenges, so I've been spending a lot of time with her, and my mother is in her 80s, and, um, she's doing

really great, but she can use a hand once in a while, you know, so it's all – al of a sudden I'm involved with my family closer than I have been, um, and it's brought up a lot of compassion. It has developed, uh, working with my sister, and being with my sister has opened up this – this, uh, compassion. (Charlie)

Others like Julie explained that they were able to just spend more time together than before.

My husband really didn't get to see me those first few, you know, the first decade of our marriage, really. I – When you're home one weekend a month or, you know, a few days here or there. Um, we had a quite a long-distance relationship. And so just being able to be home and have dinner together was really nice those, you know, the first few years after I made this transition. (Julie)

Ann didn't discuss that much change had occurred since her relationships were stable before and after her transition. Others, such as Riya and Kyle, who had some instability in their relationships before, were hopeful for better relationships in their new beginning.

Um –I think I'm more clear so people have said to me wow you – you've changed a lot — and really I hadn't changed, it's just that the stability of the vocation and the passion I had towards what I am doing now has made me happy. (Kyle)

I observed that the relationship change was an important element in everyone's transition. For those with stable relationships, the transition was easier, less stressful.

Change was worth it.

In the interviews, I was interested to know how the participants measure or know that they made the right choice. For most, the measurement was their positive feelings and emotions. They described not dreading getting up in the morning to go to work. They explained feeling fulfilled, having a good feeling inside, and being happier overall was their measure. For some, being able to make their own schedule and be more flexible, for others having passion towards their work was important.

> You know, it's 9 out of 10, probably. Is it the perfect job for the rest of my life? No. There's obviously pluses and minuses of every job. But it, it hits just about every major box for me. So yeah, it was absolutely the right move. If I had it to do over again, I absolutely would have. (Julie)

> Um, I think I'm, I, I, I've – I measure it by, uh, the passion I

think that I have.

For Juan, it is important to feel free to dream and be open to new opportunities.

> I started to have permission to have bigger dreams. Um, so I
> mean for me, my goal and my value right now is to – to have
> the roads alive... Yeah, exactly. So that's – that's a great sense of
> purpose that I have, and that is perfect for me because I can have
> all this emotional when it comes down to relating to people. And
> put it in action, you know, and having them relate with me, and
> see things for themselves. (Juan)

Finally, I asked the group, if they were to give advice to others who were considering major midlife change in their life and work, what advice would they give. Sam summed this up best for the group:

> There are trial and errors, but don't give up. I've had to make
> some, numerous changes heading me towards the direction that's
> just right for me. (Sam)

And this is indeed what I learned from the interviews that each road will be quite unique and different for each person. The road becomes clearer with movement, decisions, and choices for more meaningful work.

Summary and key learning from the interviews

Some of my research findings are consistent with the literature and yet in other areas, this research provides new insight in the experience before and after the transition which has not been covered as much in the literature to date. The research provided new insight into the experience of vocational re-alignment in midlife. This discussion is organized by stages as a way of organizing and linking the results back to the literature showing where there is agreement, or disagreement.

There were **five stages** which emerged from the collective analysis. These stages revolved around a cycle of change. This cycle started with an awareness of how unhappy the people I interviewed were in their work lives in the past. This led eventually to deep reflection and a new need for self-care and self-awareness. As a result of this, the participants described that they were more confident to move towards change although they thought the transition would be difficult. They saw the need to find a new work which would be a better alignment with their overall lives and sense of self. This cycle led to many challenges and difficult transitions. In the end, the participants described their lives as working again and, in most cases, feeling a greater sense of peace, joy, and happiness with their work and lives. Ultimately, all participants were consistent in the interviews and said their changes were worth it.

The five stages

Stage 1: The experience of "Treadmill" of Life and Work

The participants explained their situations before their change as the experience of "treadmill" of life and work. There is much support in the literature on the experiences people go through when working in jobs that carry little meaning. The results of this study, however, show that there is much variation in how people experience their own treadmill of work. Some have described this as a feeling of being unsatisfied or pondering whether their work roles make sense any longer (Hollis, 2003). Many of the participants explained their lives before as a rat race or a series of days which seemed routine and boring. This was described in the literature, as work for many was a series of deceleration and disengagement experiences (Hall & Rabinowitz, 2008) or feeling stranded or left behind (Mayer, 1978). The participants described their lives as empty and did recognize that there was something missing for them (Hollis, 2006). This tension has been described as critical for the human condition (Frankl, 1984). Therefore, the participants couldn't handle this situation for a long period of time.

Participants described their work in terms such as lacking meaning, focused on shareholders, and making money with little purpose (Sievers, 1986; Cochran, 1990). A few participants explained that the people they saw working around them seemed to be doing their jobs without the issues they had which made them feel different and alone. In the literature, there is significant support for this feeling of lack of interest or seeing meaning in one's work (Sheehy, 1995; Goldman, 2009; Lawrence-Lightfoot, 2009).

Many of the participants discussed feeling stuck and hopeless at times in their old work lives. They said there was much work to be done and long hours to do this work. They were just not sure if they were the ones to carry this out. This focus on work output and productivity towards a paycheck void of personal meaning is well supported in the literature (Csikszentmiehalyi, 1988; Langer, 1997; Rubin, 1976). The participants described their work lives before their change in fairly negative terms. For long periods of time, they felt forced to work. Today, there is support in the literature that many mid-life workers feel pressure from younger workers and continue to work in jobs that carry little meaning and no longer provide the retirement watch or 401K (Freedman, 2011). This doesn't enable an easy transition to work that they would rather do.

Several people during the interviews continued to work just to support their families but deep inside knew this could not last forever if they didn't enjoy their work (Campbell, 1968). The problem they explained was that if they worked harder the organization that they worked for kept giving them even more work. They told me this led to stress. There is also research evidence that this behavior does lead to stress and health issues later (Scott & Jaffe, 2004; Leshan, 1973). Many participants told me that they worked in their meaningless jobs probably longer than they should have (May, 1973) just because they didn't know what else to do. Some thought for a while that their best years were behind them, and this idea was supported in the literature (Raines, 1994).

Stage 2: Internal and External Triggers Pushed the Need for Change

It was interesting to hear that the participants described their inner questioning which started them down the path to change. Many discussed the feeling that something major had to change in their life. This inner questioning was also discussed in the literature (Roach, 2011; Sheehy 1995) as a period of life when perhaps a major event occurred to prompt sudden questioning. Indeed, in the interviews many discussed a job layoff, divorce, or death of a parent as the trigger that moved them into action. There is support in the literature for this re-assessment and self-appraisal (Vaillant, 1977).

May (1973) discussed the need to stand back and view one's life from a broader perspective and the people I interviewed did this. Some took time off from work, others took advantage of a break from work, and others after death of a relative or divorce used this time for new views about their life and work. I observed almost a need to be selfish at this point of their lives.

For my participants, first steps towards change happened after the external or internal triggers pushed them towards change. From my observation, the women were more sensitive to react to their inner questioning vs. men who made major moves only after some external event happened in their life.

Stage 3: Time for Reflection, Self-Awareness, and Self-Care

I found it important to discover that all participants described that at some point they felt the need to seek more meaning in their lives (Hollis, 2006). Levinson (1978) discussed the importance of questioning one's own expectations. Participants described this questioning in all the interviews. This is consistent in the literature as a process that people go through. It is also interesting to note that this questioning seemed to come as described from within and not from others or society views. As it was described in literature, this was still a period of life where, before making big changes, it was necessary to reconcile past events before moving forward (Goldman, 2009; Roach, 2011; McAdams, 1993). This need for re-examination was stressed to me during the interviews and was consistent with the literature (Bandura, 1980; Csikzentmihalyi, 1997).

Most had discussed in the interviews that when they felt that they had reached the limits of what they could accomplish in their current work (Lambley, 1995) they started questioning what they would rather do (Reisman, 1961). They described wanting to take control of their lives and to spend their energy in new ways. This is consistent with the work of McAdams (1993) and Hudson (1995) who suggested that people in midlife have a need to become more complete persons. The participants shared their feelings of suddenly reaching a conflict in their lives between their current work situation and the fact that they were getting older and thus new behavioral adjustments were required (Raines, 1994; Brammer & Abrego, 1981).

Some participants described their sudden realization that perhaps there was work that was naturally suited to them (Boldt, 1996). Those interviewed described to me the need to do work that inspired them (James, 1955; Moore, 1992). I did find a few examples in the career theories for this with the exception of social cognitive theory which assumes that cognitive factors do influence career decision making (Lent & Brown, 2011). This idea was also adapted by others (Mitchell & Kromboltz, 1996). Later, Lent & Brown (2008) suggested that the framework for making career choices needed to include linking together vocational interests. Other researchers have called this the time for claim one's place at the fire (Leider & Shapiro 2004) and to not settle for abstract work (Frankl, 1984). I was at the point of reviewing the results when I saw the momentum and confidence building for moving towards what they wanted, their dream (Toms & Toms1998; Cochran, 1990).

Some participants described the spiritual nature of a call to action in this inner reflection which was shown in the work of Hollis (2003) and Lewin (1935). The participants discussed how they went through a process of trying to figure out which work was better for them and which they would enjoy (Roach, 2011; Browning, 2007). They also discussed as was also noted in the literature (Sheehy, 1995), the need to make a difference in the world on their own terms. There is support in the literature for this self-examination (Fromm, 1994) and for many participants, it became a sole focus for some time.

This inner reflection and new perception of work (McAdams, 1993; Pepper, 1942) was represented in the ways in which the participants described their journey. This reminds me of the ways in which Jung (1957) discussed the need for storytelling as a way of interpreting events in one's life.

In the interviews, I saw that this moved the participants towards change in their lives while taking greater control (Csikszentmihalyi, 1975; Brehony, 1996). This later was discussed in more recent literature, the idea of second acts in one's life and work (Chope, 2011). The participants I interviewed were role models for what Freedman (2011) and Bateson (2010) described as a new start in one's life. This new inner reflection led those I interviewed to see the need for change although they said they knew it would not be easy.

I observed that each participant had carefully taken the time with their transitions for self-care. I also observed at this stage a commitment to change with no turning back. The participants discussed that they must change their lives and as a result have greater insight towards what they wanted to do and align much more closely with their inner self than ever before.

Stage 4: Change was Difficult

There is evidence in the literature that people get stuck and find change difficult (Levoy, 1997; Toms & Toms, 1998). In the interviews the participants were consistent in their responses with regards to their realization that change was mandatory for them despite knowing that it would be difficult. The literature is lacking in what the actual experience was like during the change in midlife to more fulfilling work. That is where in my view, this study contributes new insights.

While those interviewed did not have severe life conditions at the time which would have made change more difficult (Chope, 2006), they did experience significant reactions to the change. I discovered from my participants that they all had to make adjustments in their financial situations. Also, it was important for all participants to ensure that their transition met not only their economic needs but also their needs for peace and being content with their new choices. For all participants, this was an important step before making change. I found that the transition was easier for those who had supportive relationships. The participants discussed different ways they discovered their new vocation. For most, it was a sequence of trial and error as they didn't have a roadmap for what to do next.

I found that in the process towards change, my participants were centered around the idea of caring and protecting themselves from negative influences at this stage of their life (Toms & Toms, 1998). Many participants in my study encountered loss of friends during the transition period. Those who did not have a support preferred to stay alone. I extrapolated from the interviews that these people reached the conclusion that their life was finite and if a change was going to occur it had to be initiated by themselves (Levinson, 1978; Tamir, 1989).

Participants described this as a confusing time in their life with regards to needing to develop and yet unclear what to do (Hollis, 2006). Many had to go through professional counseling in order to draw a map for their change. For these people whom I interviewed, this was not so much a mid-life crisis; for them this was a part of normal development in the next stage of their life (Reid & Willis, 1999). This was a view expressed by other researchers (Gould, 1972; Vaillant, 1977; Tamir, 1989) who suggested that different people experienced this point of their lives in very different ways. Some were concerned how others would react or approve of their change and others did not care (Levoy, 1997).

This study provides rich new insight describing the emotional state during the transition stage. This is important because in the author's experience, many people hold back from making major life changes due to the fear of change. It is important to recognize negative emotions which are holding one back from making positive change in life.

Those I interviewed reminded me of the themes of Dante (Alighieri, 1996), that it would take a period of darkness before new clarity appeared when going through change in midlife.

Stage 5: A New Beginning

Recent researchers (Lawrence-Lightfoot, 2009) have noted that major change in midlife is a good opportunity for exploring new possibilities where to align one's passions and interests. These possibilities lead to new work opportunities that can enable more meaning and joy.

Career theory does not pay much attention to the topic of what occurs after a shift to more fulfilling work. Application of social cognitive theory and decision making theory (Tiedeman & O'Hara, 1963; Heppner & Krauskopf, 1987) suggests that one's career is a series of decisions along one's life timeline. This is also supported by the recent work of Shoffner (2011) who notes that decision making and indecision are close to these psychological and social cognitive factors.

I discovered from the interviews that the participants at some point realized that work was a major part of their life and they had no intention of ever retiring. They no longer considered retirement as an option which is consistent with newer research of Corbett (2006) who suggests many are taking a new anti-retirement position in midlife. This is consistent with other studies (e.g., International research team, 1987) which suggested that people want to keep working if the opportunity is there to do so. The homepage of AARP (n.d.) reflects the growing trend of working longer for those in their second half of life. This study gives specific feedback and data around the factors which the participants said were important to consider as they kept working. It is interesting that while recent literature discusses the importance of working with meaning in one's second half, there is little data which also discusses the significant challenges which occur. This study adds rich new personal accounts of the difficulty when changing one's work later in life even if for new purpose and meaning.

The participants expressed to me a new sense of freedom and meaning around their work and no longer questioned the value of their work. This was expressed in the literature as well for those who would seek meaning making change in their lives (Csikszentmihalyi, 1990; Evans & Bartolome, 1981). They did say that they would never consider going back to the work which they were doing before. Some of these participants did describe their work as a calling, while others were unsure but expressed they were happier in their work then before because this was their choice (Halberstam, 2000).

Those interviewed were consistent when they said they could continue the new type of work they were doing for a long period of time because it was more inner directed then before (Scott & Jaffe, 2004). This supports the work of Becker (1971) who suggested that our self-esteem depends on our inner newsreel. Finally, the participants said, their work was finally aligned with their passions and what made them happy (Csikszentmihalyi, 1997).

This study adds new data describing both the thought process, as well as emotional and psychological steps that might occur for those making the transition in midlife from work which is stale and meaningless to work which better fits one's view of self, is more fulfilling and brings happiness.

Conclusions

The experience of these eight participants in many areas was consistent with the literature. Recent literature tends to focus on the positive benefits of recreating one's work later in life. This study also identifies in greater detail the challenges and significant issues that people can encounter when approaching such change.

The experience of participants of being bored and stuck in their work lives, while not unusual, does become a marker which those in midlife should pay attention to and not ignore. It can be easy to push aside these feelings and continue to work in jobs which provide little meaning and joy. For the participants in this study, it became critical not to ignore these signals and instead move to a deeper self-reflection, looking inward for new direction. One of the important findings of this study is that this inner search for meaning in one's work in midlife is both healthy and important for self-growth. Ignoring this could lead to other issues which not only affect the person, but also their family as well and, at a macro level, the society. As people ignore their developmental needs, they may not be as satisfied with life and those around them. Thus, in this cycle of change as learned in this study, paying attention to self-care and better self-alignment at this point of life is critical if a person wants to experience more out of work and life.

This study shows that the change to more fulfilling work is not easy and there will be many challenges. It takes both sacrifice and courage to take this journey into new roads not traveled. There will be trade-offs needed. But for those mid-life adults seeking greater peace, joy, and harmony with their work, this pursuit is needed. The results shown here suggest that mid-life adults who do take greater control of their life and work will find a deeper purpose about their lives, greater meaning about their work, and internal happiness.

The participants in this study discovered that, as a result of change, new possibilities and opportunities emerged. As a result, this led to greater self-confidence, sense of direction, and new beginnings. It would be wise to not wait for major life events to make these changes, but often it is the triggers in one's life which bring to the forefront the need for a second look at what may not be working well in one's life and work.

Additionally, this study pointed out that having strong relationships before major transition made the transition easier. For others, successful work change in midlife to greater meaning doesn't always bring better relationships. This study also pointed out that based on a person's economic situation, making major life and work change later in the second half of life is quite unique to each person. This study shows that throughout and after the transition, much trial and error will be required and for those without the needed financial resources for everyday living. And, as a result, this process will be very difficult.

These participants shared a valuable lesson which showed that change can be challenging, lonely, and fearful. But it is the necessary road to travel on if the adults are willing to explore and eventually create a work life which best fits them for the middle part of their lives and beyond.

It is important to note that with this study there were certain limitations to be considered. For example, it is possible that with a group of people who had different cultural, social, economic, and experience base backgrounds the results might be different. There are many social factors which influence people's decisions especially when it comes to their work. For many people it may seem too risky to make major work change without secure new opportunities in place. These factors were excluded from this research. Also excluded was the general state of the economy at the time and how this influenced the participants' decision making.

For some adults who made such change in their work lives and had negative experiences, the results of such a study would also be different. The results might also vary with a group of people who have had more rewarding careers and as a result have different experience in their midlife.

It may not be necessary for all adults to make such radical change in their work in mid-life especially if they enjoy their work. So, in this study much depends on the specific backgrounds and current life experiences of those interviewed. Still, there are some factors which can be examined from this study and the literature which may be common for many mid-life adults seeking more meaning and fulfillment in their work lives.

Application of this Study for the Readers

This book and research will be useful for therapists such as psychologists and social workers who assist clients with various issues that may have underlining connections to their work unhappiness. They can compare the experience that my participants went through to their clients' situations. Then, this research will bring new insights for corporate managers to help them understand the deeper needs for development of mid-life adults with regards to their work. This research will also help career and life coaches to assist their clients to get clear about their plans and the steps required to achieve their life and work goals.

Additionally, this research will be useful for career counselors and educational organizations which offer training programs for career development. This research will be interesting for organizations that study aging and who offer various training programs and publications for mid-life adults. Finally, this research will be a good guide for those mid-life adults going through the actual experience of major change while seeking more meaning and fulfillment in their work.

What We Can Learn From These Stories

The Experience of the "Treadmill" of Life and Work

How about you?

Can you describe when you have felt stuck in your work?

How did you know this? What signals did you notice?

What did you do about this?

My advice

Start to pay attention to when you feel stuck at work. Stop and reflect. What are the reasons? What changes can you make to enable you to feel more excited, more passionate about your work? Which new work would you rather do and why?

Work doesn't bring satisfaction.

This is important because when we don't enjoy our work, we are wasting away our lives. You will spend more hours working in your life than any other activity. Shouldn't this be the highest priority?

My advice

Spend some time thinking what you are most interested in. Which are your best abilities and which are you also motivated to do? See where these align as it is the intersection of abilities and interests where what I call vocational passion can be found.

Feeling disconnected with others

This is usually a result of not enjoying your work. As a result, you look around and everyone else seems to enjoying their work. You wonder what's wrong with you. The reality is nothing is wrong at all. You are just not fitting in and it is probably time for a change.

My advice

Start to build a support network with people who are doing what you would rather do. This can be a networking group, an online group, a class or others who you get together with. Find others who share your deep interests and this will energize you. Find a few people who are doing exactly what you want to do next. They will give you helpful advice. Finally, find a mentor who is an expert in the field you also want to contribute to. This can be a real person or even a book you can read. This person will inspire you to greatness!

Work was endless and carried little meaning

I observed this with those who I interviewed. While just a job gives us objectives and things to do in the second half of life, it is more important whether your work brings coherence and meaning.

My advice

Does it make sense to you why you do the work which you do? This is coherence. Does your work bring you meaning? If not, which work would? No one from HR will run up to you on Monday morning to ask you this. It must come from deep within you.

Internal and External Triggers Pushed the Need for Change

There are triggers which occur often in our life and we usually don't pay attention to them and what they mean.

My advice

Step back and reflect. What internal or external triggers have occurred for you lately? These triggers can present themselves in different ways. It may be a big event like a layoff, medical scare or a divorce. It may just be small events such as boredom day in and day out, a short temper or just feeling a little down all the time. These triggers present a good time to take action.

Divorce, layoff, death of a relative.

These are examples of big trigger events. They shake up your world. Some people just feel bad and move on with the same behavior, the same daily routines. This, however, is a good time to take some time and reflect about your life, where you have been, where you are and where you are going.

My advice

If any of the above has happened to you although I hope not, take the time to ask yourself what action you might take as a result of this major event in your life that would enable you to find deeper happiness in your life and work.

Sudden realization of the need to change

It can be a scary process to realize you must make big change in your life. Remember though that it is big change which causes new opportunities to create a life and work which works better for you.

My advice

Write down what needs to change in your life now and why? This is a good first step.

Internal push for change

Many times what you may feel inside is a symptom of a bigger challenge. These emotions you are feeling may be connected to this need for something new, more exciting, meaningful in your life. Don't ignore these feelings. They are your feelings and they are real.

My advice

Take action! Many days it can be easy to stay busy and ignore the most important emotions and feelings which come up throughout the day. This is your inner guidance system, your own GPS telling you this is time to change direction now. What new direction do you need to take in your life now and why? If you know the why, the how will come.

Time for Reflection, Self-Awareness, and Self-Care

Rarely do we take the time unless there is a crisis which forces us to step back and reflect deeply about our lives. As we become more self-aware we are then better able to take care of our needs and do what is right for us.

My advice

Don't wait for your crisis to hit. Take a few hours now or better a few days and go away to a place in nature where you can be alone. Think deeply about your life, your purpose, and where you most want to make a contribution now and why. Think deeply about what is most important to you and how you might develop new goals to align closer to your personal values. This time off will be the best investment you will ever make and it will affect you in a positive way as well as all those around you for years to come.

Going through healing.

Many times during a big crisis in our lives, we will require time alone. During this time we are quiet, we feel down, lonely and we think about the loss which we just encountered. This is normal and a healthy part of moving towards feeling better.

My advice

When you have encountered a loss, don't ignore your feelings and the healing which needs time and space to recover. Life will be good again if you are patient.

Needed to step back and reflect

Going through a crisis requires a slowdown. Time is needed to think through what has occurred and what you might do next as a result. This might result in little or major change.

My advice

Take time; get rid of some activities in your life which are not adding value. Think about what types of changes might be healthy for you now to make. Imagine how your life and work might be better if you took these steps. With a new vision of your desired state, you will gain new energy and momentum to move forward again.

Exploring new opportunities.

Imagine yourself as an explorer who will travel to new areas of interests which you have not been before. Be open to new learning, new experiences, and new relationships.

My advice

Make a plan to explore! Figure out what you want to explore, who you want to meet, what you want to do. Imagine this as a field trip except this time you don't need a permission slip from anyone! It often only takes one new experience or change or encounter and new learning to change your own perspective of life and work! I'll be waiting to read your trip report!

Change was Difficult

If changing one's work was easy then everyone would do this each they lost interest in their work. The reality shows that change is hard, especially a big change. One has to be prepared to make tradeoffs, take risks, and have courage and venture into new territory when making big changes in work. This takes a strong network, good support system and stronger emotions to defeat external opinions which might not agree with your change.

My advice

Seek to make big change. It is only through big change in one's work where there can be a significant shift in joy and passion. What big change can you make now?

Unknown path

Changing one's work in midlife can feel threatening at many levels. But it is this unknown path which is better traveled down then the more familiar path which has ended you up where you are, perhaps right now. Plus, when traveling down a new path, there are sure to be new experiences, new visions, and new ideas which appear. Which might be a better path for you right now and why?

My advice

Seek a new path which is both unknown and yet exciting to you. As a result, you will find your own pot of gold at the end of the rainbow.

Loss of friends.

From my experience and research, there is a good chance one might lose some friends along the way to a fuller, more joyful work life. This is because many people prefer to not take the risk to grow because they are afraid to lose what they have. Friends can become resentful that you made this change without them. Just know that good friends will support you with whatever path you decide to take. Otherwise, it is better to leave them behind.

My advice

Don't be afraid to let go of the relationships which are holding you back and don't support where you want to go next. Not letting go is both unhealthy and will not move you forward.

You will end up finding better relationships which better support you in this next phase of life and work.

Trial and error.

As I found with the people I interviewed, there is much trial and error involved when changing from work without meaning to joyful work.

My advice

Be prepared to try out different approaches, be patient with yourself and you will soon find the combination which works just right for you!

Financial hurdles

Money is a complicated area. You have to be the one to determine how much you need to make in your new joyful work. There are tradeoffs and this will not come easy. Be prepared in fact for some difficult times. If you are not prepared to give up at least for a while your current lifestyle to make this transition, then, this is not the right time for you to consider big change.

My advice

Making big change requires a big lifestyle change for many people for a few years. This is hard for some people. I suggest considering tapping into whatever resources you have including your retirement. After all, why not use this money now so you never have to retire and instead do what you enjoy!

Better sense of self

As I spoke to those who I interviewed, I sensed a renewed confidence and better self-awareness. They felt better about themselves as a result of deciding and then taking action.

My advice

If you are unhappy with your work, the best action now to take is to make a decision and take action (both are required) to make big change. This will be the best reward you can give yourself.

Change was worth it.

I learned from my interviews that all participants thought the change was worth it and there was no second guessing or wanting to go back to what they had done before.

My advice

Once you decide you are going to explore new options, don't turn back despite what others might say or think about what you are doing.

Better relationships

It was interesting to learn from the people I interviewed how their relationships had improved. I observed that this was a result of making positive change in their life and work which resulted in feeling better about those around them.

My advice

Know that in taking positive steps to improve the quality and experience of your life and work will result in better relationships for you as well!

A New Beginning

I observed that the people I interviewed experienced new joy and happiness after their transitions. The transition itself was the hardest work which they had ever done. In the end, it was well worth it and never once did any of the people I interviewed considered going back to what they were doing before.

My advice

Envision what the rest of your life could look like with a big change in your work. With this vision of new possibilities you gain new insight, new energy, and new momentum to move forward.

Self-assessment for the reader

Take a piece of paper and answer these questions for yourself to assess which stage you might be at in your life as a step towards more joy in your own work!

Stage 1: The experience of "Treadmill" of Life and Work

Can you think of a time when you felt like you were on a treadmill in your life and work?

What did it feel like?

How did you know that you were on a treadmill?

How did this treadmill affect your life and your relationships?

Stage 2: Internal and External Triggers Pushed the Need for Change

Which triggers have occurred for you in your life which gave you pause and the opportunity to step back and reflect about your life and your work?

Were these triggers internal or external?

What did you do as a result?

What could you do?

Stage 3: Time for Reflection, Self-Awareness, and Self-Care

Have you taken the time after a trigger to reflect about your life and work?

What process did you use?

If not, what steps could you take?

What possibilities might occur if you took the time to self-reflect?

What would self-care look like for you now?

Stage 4: Change was Difficult

What would be difficult for you now if you decided to change your work in a big way to seek more joy?

What would this change look like?

How would this change affect your financial state?

What adjustments could you make in your financial state, your relationships, and your lifestyle to make this change work?

What would be the overall impact to the quality of your life now if you made big change in your life and work?

Stage 5: A new Beginning

Can you describe how this would make you feel and why?

How would a new beginning benefit you now and those around you?

What are the major three lessons you learned from this book?

Epilogue

My goal with this book and my research was to provide ideas, inspiration and incentive for you to examine and explore your own life and work now. As a result of this exploration, I believe the second half of your life will be filled with more joy, more passion and greater happiness. As a result, this will affect you and all those around you. This change will not be easy. In fact, it will be the hardest thing you will ever do.

But in the end you will be grateful you made the change. Your life will be more authentic and you will make a greater difference in the world. We would all benefit from this!

I wish you the best success in your journey and don't forget to enjoy the process. This journey will provide the deepest insight and self-awareness in your life that you have ever experienced. When this occurs, be sure to celebrate and write me to tell me about it.

Warm regards,

Dr. Craig Nathanson

June, 2013, Petaluma, Ca USA

The Interviews

(Question by question as they were asked)

1. Can you describe your life situation when you identified or discovered and decided to follow a new vocational path?

> **Julie:** I worked for profit organizations. I had spent about 20 years as a corporate human resources, employee relations trained leader.
>
> And really, it was a very clear mark in time for me. It was, um, summer of, uh, after, following a very large acquisition, where I was the HR leader for that acquisition.
>
> …. And finishing up this acquisition in the summer, it was the month of July, it was also my birthday month. And I started to really get clear with myself that because I had done a really nice job and gotten a lot of accolades on this acquisition, that knowing this organization, it meant that I was gonna be on the hook for more of the same.
>
> Yep. I was gonna be, you know, tapped on the shoulder for other initiatives. And, frankly, I had allowed myself in a lot of life, um, for the last few years. And so that summer, uh, literally the

month of my birthday, decided I wasn't gonna be continuing in the corporate path.

❧

Janet: And so, um, working at a regular J-O-B, it was, um, confining. I felt trapped. I didn't like somebody else telling me when I can eat and when I can't eat.

And when I can do this or that. So, um, I found it very confining.

Uh, yeah, well, I think – anxiety I think would be a good, uh, summary.

❧

Juan: I was living with a lot of anxiety — and, um, trying to make things right, um, but very bored. Um, uh, feeling a little bit, um, guilty. I wouldn't say guilty, but, uh, not having a very strong image — of myself. Not – not really, um, uh, seeing myself as someone with, um, consistency, but integrity. Um, and I think a little insecure.

It was like that. That was, um, and morbid. I think I didn't have – I didn't have observations for the future.

Riya: Um, it had a more singular, uh, focus, you know, what I spent my time, and so not only was I a little bit bored, but I had this, um – a depression coming on because my soul was not being fulfilled.

⚬⚬⚬

Kyle: Uh, highly stressful, um, mainly a lot of anxiety, um, although – [Laughs] It was uh, my life was uh, very stressful, a lot of anxiety, um, um, money worries, we, we always had enough money. We always made good money but for some reason, I still harbored a lot of internal fear because uh, it just wasn't, I just didn't feel stable.

2. What lead you to know that something needed to change in your vocational life? What was the trigger for you?

Julie: Uh, yeah. The final trigger was, um, you know, that, that acquisition closed out and I realized, um, you know, that was on a Friday, and I realized on Monday that I was getting lined right back up for another project just like that, without any breathing room or recovery space. Um, and that, you know, financially, I was in a place, you know, after having given 20 years in corporate America, that I could take some risks. Um, I was questioning, honestly, whether I needed to get out of HR, whether I needed to get out of corporate America, or whether I needed to get out of both and just kind of start fresh. And it was a whole, like, you know, rethinking my identity because I'm an HR gal.

Um, so I did. I, I literally walked away. I gave notice, um, you know, on the heels of a potentially very large promotion and, um, went to work for the – I just completely changed of – Um, took a job as a career adviser at, uh, at a local University here. And I realize now in hindsight that that was really my own year of self-reflection. I was there to advise students, but really I was advising myself throughout that year.

Wow, what, what could I be? What could I be if this label wasn't attached, you know, squarely to my forehead? Um, if I wasn't living behind this, you know, title? What, what are those other things I'm interested in and, and truly how do I want to spend the rest of my career?

❧

Sam: Yeah. It's definitely one of those things where I, I just felt that I was gonna get back on the treadmill one more time, and I couldn't do it anymore, and I wanted to live a more authentic life, enjoying what am I doing and not just working to make ends meet. And even that was not something that was reliable. I'm being told, "Doing a great job, but you're making too much money." Commission cuts, having jobs I had outsourced offshore, downsized, reengineered regardless of my performance. And of course if the company was having a tough time, I could get laid off for not making, making quota. And I had felt just the working was like looking for work all the time.

You go in to – Even except I was getting a commission check, you know? It just – And I'd been – Just couldn't, I just couldn't do that anymore.

And I, and I wanted to follow my calling.

❧

Janet: And, um, and then I just started reading, and it sparked something in me. And I thought that sounded really appealing, and I just – Um, I wanted to have the freedom to do what I wanted and do something that I loved instead of, uh, being pigeonholed into, you know, "You don't have a degree, you don't have this and that, this and that, so you can only do this and you can only make this much."

So the trigger was the freedom and independence, really.

❦

Juan: Uh, [laughs]. I think – I think was the – the humiliation.

Um, four – four times I think being laid off.

Um, I – I told myself, you know, I don't wanna be humiliated anymore.

Right, and, uh, what happened was that when I was laid off for the fourth time, I was already doing work review. I remember that – And then after that, um, you know, there was that problem with work – With, you know, some people that worked with me.

Um, that lead to my dismissal.

So I didn't wanna go through the experience anymore.

❦

Riya: I had two triggers. One was one morning. I had to be on an early morning meeting. But I had to get my car serviced, and I — you know, juggling a bunch of things, so I had this early appointment at the – at the service center, and I went up there and dropped off the car and ran to catch a cab just so I could get back home to get on the morning meeting, and I whacked myself in the head in the third eye.

[Giggles]. And it – and it started bleeding, and so that was a wake-up call, like try – you know, was it really worth all that just to get on to a silly meeting

And then, finally, when, you know, I thought I had put all this effort into adding creativity into my work and being – doing a big contribution that I thought was creative, a creative way to contribute just – and I had tried to work with, um, you know, the organizational development people and the human resources people and all that to make –the work life better and, uh, ranking and rating came along, and I was – so it looked like I was gonna be demoted.

And that seemed – it just seemed like it didn't fit the situation, and I didn't wanna play anymore.

⊂⊛⊃

Charlie: It was something very specific in a very specific time and place. My father had passed away, and I was headed east on Speedway Boulevard in Tucson; my father had passed away a couple of weeks earlier, and I was like, "Wow," all of a sudden in this one moment I thought, "Man, I'm gonna die too." And in that very moment, I – I said, "I've got to do something about my life," and I made a commitment to myself to take six months off to travel and take pictures, which is what I was most passionate about.

3. Can you describe in more details how your typical day looked like before you made the decision to follow a new vocational path?

Julie: Oh, my goodness. Um –

Typical day would've started at 6:00 a.m. with East Coast or international conference calls. Sometimes they were in the middle of the night because I was doing international work. Um, often travel. I traveled about 70 to 80 percent of the time. Um, and nonstop meetings, nonstop pressure, nonstop firefighting. Um, a lot of emotion because I was in HR, obviously. A lot of people issues that, that are pretty draining.

Um, I'm an introvert by nature and I didn't realize at the time how draining that really was for me.

Um, I was leading a large team. They were scattered all over, so I never really had that, um, never really had a feeling of having it all together because there was just so much going on and so quickly.

I never felt like I could be completely successful. It was just kind of spiraling, um, it was so much all the time.

And often working, you know, weekends. And the, the workday never really ended. You could, you know, you could never really call it done.

❧

Sam: Uh, get up in the morning. Um, take a shower, have a cup of coffee, a little breakfast and vitamins. Go to work. Come home, eat dinner, go to bed. I mean, just doing the same thing over and over again. So you wind up – Yeah, good, caught up, okay. If the bills were paid, at least I was treading water, but wasn't feeling any sense of personal fulfillment.

❧

Janet: You wake up at 6:00. You go to work at, be at work at 8:00 or 8:30 and, um, you know, and you work all day. Um, you go – I went to the gym at – After work. And then I came home, I had a couple of hours of, uh, to eat and to, um, just, you know, catch up on stuff, and then I would go to bed and I would repeat it. Day after day after day after day. A rat in a maze.

❧

Juan: Well, um, I was, you know, the moment that I left the car to walk into the office, I could feel the anxiety and my – my breathing was… was different. I was breathing differently. Um, and the experience of walking into an office was the same experience of walking to another planet. Uh, in a sense that people were aliens. I didn't have that sense of – of relatedness with people.

Um, I – I thought that we were very different –

Yeah. I could see myself different and isolated. And I would see that everybody was – I – I – I thought that everybody was like that.

That nobody was comfortable. It was an environment of – of – of – of solitude. I don't know. Solitude, distance.

❦

Riya: Typical day - get in very early, um, because your part of the development – manufacturing development.

So there's the manufacturing component, so you have the manufactured floor where tools are, you know, have to be on 24 by 7, and – the people are really hyper if anything's going wrong. ….
And then, from there, you're following any kind of problems with

the product that you have an overview of as a product engineer. And no – no moments in there to actually do anything [sighs] creative or long term or, you know, preventative. And when I actually started to take time to do that, that's when I wasn't seen as being as productive. And lots of coffee, lots of espresso, people yell in meet – yelling at each other in the meetings, people yelling at each other across the cubicle, you know?

4. What is your new vocation today?

Julie: I'm a non-profit executive. I lead a non-profit healthcare organization.

❦

Sam: Ah, I'd say I'm a teacher or a college instructor.

❦

Janet: I would say I'm the strong copy quarterback at Winning Proof. And that is my title, and that is what I do, and that defines me, and I have, you know, when you talk about your job, it's like "Yeah, and I do this and blah blah blah." Now it gave me a bigger – And it gave me an excitement. You can see my eyes light up.

❦

Juan: Well, I – I think, [laughs], I think, um, I'm still in the process, but you can call me, uh, uh, entrepreneur.

To the idea of well, there's something else that I'm perfectly fit and made for.

And I think the cool thing was that my vision of the world changed as well because I cannot see anybody, um, as, um, as – as – I don't know how to say the right word, but I'm capable. I can see someone that is unfit to something, but absolutely fit to something else.

⁂

Riya: I would say, I have two types of work. I have two gigs that I do. One is I do, um, technical consulting for patent litigations.

And the – and the other is I do healing arts work, including teaching, uh – I'm teaching physics to the – to healers.

⁂

Kyle: Uh, so, so it's kind of evolving a little bit. Uh, we are um, we're actually in essence money managers that use real estate as a vehicle.

And, uh, we do all different types of strategies in real estate investment.

❧

Charlie: Now I'm extremely passionate about the book that I'm writing right now. So now I'm working on refining the ability to teach – to use my voice and to teach other people to use their voice to connect with – to heal themselves by connecting with their interior reality through sound. Does that make sense?

❧

Ann: Um, helping people, uh, make money from home simply and easily. Have more time for fun.

5. How did you discover your new vocation?

Julie: Uh, it was interesting. Once, I shed the label and, um, I took that year, kinda academic year, um, as this career adviser, um, it became really obvious that I was not going back to corporate America. Um, but I still loved HR. And, um, the dream job just landed in my lap. Truly, once, once I opened my eyes, um, within, within days this dream job landed in my lap, and I've never looked back.

❧

Janet: I wanted to marry my love of football, NFL football, with my love of writing.

And I had seen – In fact, I'd – Lately I've seen my grade school report cards, and every single grade said that I excelled in writing. And that was just, you know, I didn't know it at the time. But, um, that's what I wanted to do. I've always been a natural writer and, um, I had spent a lot of time in my room, um, as a child.

And then, but as a grownup, I wanted to marry my love of the two. And I thought, "Oh my gosh, this, this is it."

I was propelled into the patent litigation because the universe sort of kicked me out of what I was doing, and I needed something quickly to pay the rent, and I went – went on craigslist.

⌘

Riya: Um, sent out a resume and heard back the next day. So it felt like just a divine push. Um — and then –and then I –I was tutoring which is part-time work. …So when I was exploring the "soul" part, the – you know, the – the – the creative work, The Artist's Way, I – I did yoga teacher training and started studying Shamanic practices, and so this was a, you know, continuation return to – to that. So I was – you – I wasn't employed full time, and I had time to finish this training in energy medicine and heal-ing arts and continued and have continued as I have the patent litigation because there's all this flexibility, and I have a lot of – I give it a lot of respect and value.

⁓

Kyle: Uh, this was – real estate was something I was always interested in. It's funny because when I was 20 years old, my mom was a real estate agent. I bought my first property. And, at that point at the table, I remember I didn't know anything. I was a 20-year-old kid sitting around the table with lawyers and real estate agents and, and it was so exciting to me that I never did it again for 30 years [laughs] or 25 years. It was so exciting I'm like I walked out of that office after I signed all these paperwork which I didn't know – you know, it's just, I was basically a teen-ager.

And I bought a house. My mom had helped me buy this house and uh, I was working of course but, but uh, I always had that at the back of my head like that was really cool when I did that, you know? And for – and I always thought about it. Then, uh, I watched the show called Flip This House…Uh, you know, I got handed the divorce papers out of the blue and, and that was it.

That was the straw. Does that make sense?

⚜

Charlie: Well, going back to my big trip through Latin America, I finished that trip and I wrote a book. I had – along the way - I was uploading photos and short stories to the web. I was very passionate about photography and I got into writing in a big way, writing very short little stories. They were easily consumable on the web, and I got back and I had this body of work, and I thought, "Oh, I could – I could turn this into a book," and I – which I did, and, um, it too knew a lot longer than I thought, but I – I created a – I wrote and produced – published a book, and then I was out doing talks to promote the book, and I had created a slideshow using my photography, which I was very proud of, and inspirational quotes.

⚜

Ann: Well, um, when I decided to make the switch, I went to work for a marketing company, and they were, uh, launching in Australia. ...So I went over to Australia and, um – and it was very difficult. The office wasn't set up. We only had three weeks, and the office wasn't even set up the first week, and no products, no brochures. So it was quite a challenge. But I'm a determined person, so of course, I wasn't going to go over there and not succeed. So I did. I literally walked door to door to over 200 business and, um, met the challenge. So my income was going to be doubled. But while I was over there, somebody that I, uh, uh, highly respected in business sent me an email, you know, uh, sharing with me about an internet based, um, business opportunity.

Um, and when I saw that, I thought, oh my gosh, this is incredible.

It didn't depend as much on other people. So, um, yeah, that's – that's what happened. So when I got back, that's what I did. I just started studying that. And – and, um, then I, you know, developed a little system and wrote my books.

6. Can you describe how it feels when you are doing your new work as the main focus of your day?

Julie: Um, most days I can't wait to get here. Um, and funny enough, when I'm off or away on vacation or something, I miss the people I'm with, I work, I get to work with. So I come back to work very much having missed being here. Um, it's more than just a job. It's, it's a calling, it's – I know it sounds a little cheesy, probably, but you know, but I'm making a difference. We're taking care of patients in the Valley that don't have other options for, you know, healthcare for those, um, that may not, that may have to go without.

❧

Sam: Oh, it feels great. It's, I – And also because it feels good because I am, uh, I'm doing what I enjoy doing, which to me it seems like – I'm teaching psychology classes that I took 30, 35 years ago. But somehow that material is retained, and I can talk about it. Talk on these classics extemporaneously for four hours and set up activities and uh, um, uh, discussions and things like that without having to refer – It's amazing how much material from my 20s I've retained going into my 50s. Uh, so I'm – Also, I'm very happy 'cause I wake up, I don't have what we talked about years ago is that I don't wake up and think about where do I – You know, I have to get up, I have to go to work. I – Yeah, I have to go to work. I have to get out of my bedroom, make a cup of coffee, and then walk into my home office and do my online classes and creating or, as I am today, prepping for tonight's – I have a lesson plan to do after this, but that only takes me about an hour, hour and a half.

❧

Janet: It's energizing. You can make your own schedule. You can work out in the morning if you want to, uh, when nobody else is.

And you start – You know, and I have a structure. I'm naturally structured and naturally, uh, organized in, you know, in life.

And kind of, you know, predictable, I guess. Some people would call I'm boring. But I don't think of it as, as that.

But, um, I structure my day the way I want to, and I start work at a certain time. Um, I take lunch and I go on, you know, from there. I work until, you know, take a little break in the afternoon and the early evening, and then I work until, I don't know, probably 8:00, 8:30 at night.

But it's a joy.

❦

Juan: So what I have today that I didn't have three years ago is that I have dreams, right, so I have plans, I have something that I wake up in the morning and my future gives my presence.

You know what I mean?

❦

Riya: – explore the day, although I do spend time every day sitting and being in stillness which just makes everything go beautifully.

But – so – but I – I'm – I don't have to drag myself out of bed. I often sleep as long as I need to, and then I'm awake when I need to be.

Even if I set an alarm, I'm awake a little bit before it, naturally, um, and so I feel excited about whatever's to come that day, or it's not excited. You know, I don't mean – you don't have to have, uh – that – you don't have to be on alert to – to be, um, anticipating an – an interesting day, uh, of a day full of beauty, a day full of, um, heartfelt communication with people, um, a day that you solve some puzzles and have a little, you know, fun [giggles].

❧

Kyle: Feels great.

It feels so good. I mean, I'm, you know, uh, it, but it's more, it's actually turned into more than just the, the vocation.

Uh, it's actually been more of a cleansing of my inside as well.

But, the vocation is in a catapult has been a big part of that.

So, it, it was actually releasing a lot of negative energy that had built up through those, especially those ten stagnant years.

Charlie: I've never been more – at this moment in my life, I've never been more passionate about and excited and thrilled about what I'm doing with my life, and that's saying a lot because I've done a lot of fun stuff, you know? And, uh, and I don't know, it's like – the thing on Speedway Boulevard and making that big shift, that was a pretty big – that was a pretty big, um, turning point for me, because it sort of broke from mainstream conceptual reality, and cultural reality, and went off on this adventure into foreign cultures and out of the comfort zone, and out of the culture, and ever since then, I have been on a similar – I mean, my path has been twisty and turny, but it's always been following my passion.

⟳

Ann: It's fantastic because the thing is that, you know, I'm now in a position, um, that, you know, we live very comfortably. And we live, you know, actually rather simply, which is what I prefer. I'm really not into things, you know. I'd rather, you know, rent them than, you know, have to worry about, you know, buying things and storing them and taking care of them and managing them and all that. So, uh, it's wonderful because my time is totally my own. I absolutely love it. We – I don't work hard all day. You know, I set my – it has taken a few years to get into this position to where I have the – you know, before, when I first started out, of course, I was working, you know, long hours and, um, you know, daily at it.

But I loved it. I was doing what I loved. And so it didn't feel like work, and it was very exciting and to see the progress and so on. And of course, now I've got it set up to where I don't have to work hard. My time is my own. I do travel a lot, and, um, you know, I can still conduct my business wherever I go very simply and easily just literally on a few hours a week. And it's wonderful. I can work more if I want to, but I don't have to. And it's – it's a very, very good feeling.

7. Had this change altered any of your life goals? If so, in what ways?

Julie: Oh, completely altered them. I'll never – I know today that I will never go back to, um, a large corporation.

I know that I'll never go back to for-profit funding. Um, my heart is in this work. Even if it's not this organization, which I hope it is, but even if it's not, um, it – My heart is in the non-profit sector, and I see such a need for, um, talent. I see such a need for, you know, partnerships and have gifts that I can give here.

Janet: Uh, my life goals, I'd probably have, have changed them in the fact that, you know, when you're in a job, you say "Okay, I want to be a – Make more money." Or "I want to be a, in a manager position." Or "I want to do this or that within the company." And again, that pigeonhole word. You're kind of pigeonholed. You have to wait till somebody quits, dies, moves, or something to be in certain spots in the company. Now it is all about my life.

⧈

Riya: I think that what I was doing before just didn't align with my life goals.

If I look at – if I look at things I wrote before I quit the big company I was working for – and even, you know, my musings when I was 18, 19, 20, 21 – 22, in my journals, I – this is what I was aspiring to.

⧈

Kyle: Uh, changed or altered my life goals, yep. My life goals have evolved. I guess you could say.

You know, my goals are not all about – you know, at first, at first you think your goals are about money.

And then after you start achieving a little bit, you realize that oh, no, it's not about the money. It's about, you know, having my time.

And freedom of limitation, you know, is really what my goals had turned out to be.

⤜⤛

Charlie: Yeah, I'm just trying to think how I would articulate that, and – and, um, you know, back when I was doing cosmetic dentistry, I was very passionate about that, and I was – I was fairly good at it. I had kind of a natural gift for it, and it wasn't about the money for me, even though cosmetic dentistry is a – usually it's top-dollar for the high-ticket item, and an easy way for a dentist to make money. That's not why I did it. I did it because I loved it and I had this talent, and I knew that it made a difference in people's lives. And it's sort of like the money was a byproduct of it. So there have been times where I focused on, "Oh, I really want to find a way to make a lot of money." And I've always sort of – it's always been a little bit of a dead-end to a certain extent, and I've always had to make a detour from that path, and then when I found something that I was really passionate about, it's like that's when everything flowed.

8. Could you have made this choice earlier in your life?

Julie: I don't think I was self-aware enough.

I don't think I knew what would really feed my soul. Um, the first part of my career I was much more focused on paying off student loans, you know, the mortgage, the kids, all of those real-life things that you, you know, get your life started.

Um, I don't regret having had that experience because it gave me a fantastic foundation for the second half of my career. Um, I don't think I would've been able to make this shift. And financially it would've been tougher because obviously these organizations can't, you know, pay what we're making in the corporate sector.

ℝ

Sam: And, uh, it took a while – I didn't realize that – Maybe 'cause I thought being a academic or being a teacher was something that was too easy in 20s and I wanted to take on something more challenging. But really sometimes the path of least resistance in life is better than, than, you know, trying to climb Mount Everest.

ℝ

Janet: No. I didn't have the experience, the maturity, the knowledge.

Um, to, to make it. I didn't know that the options were even available.

Until I was in a, an early 40s, mid-40s level. So I didn't even know – That wasn't even my mindset. Is that you go to school, you graduate, you get a job, and you know, the traditional career path. So, um, I don't think so, no.

❧

Juan: Um, oh yeah, absolutely. I think if I had some guidance –

– I think. If I had some guidance and, uh, I think there's a huge gap, huge, huge gap in – in – and I thought about it, in the – in the educational system as an overall. I can't say exactly in the US because I don't know. My – my, you know, my – my education was all in Brazil, but people go through, um, a lot of things in life and they have their –

– ideas of themselves and, you know, this and that, um, but they don't have the clarity — of their strengths, where they excel.

❧

Riya: I don't think so, because I still was finishing the work of the student and the, um, acquiring that – a little bit of power through identity, and that was – before you, you know, dissolve the ego, you have to one up.

❧

Kyle: Um, yes. Uh, well, I mean, I don't know, that's a good, it's a tough, it's a little bit of a tough question to answer. I guess yeah, of course you could have made them. Could I have, would I have made them? Uh, because of the situation I am, I mean, it's evidence that I didn't. So, uh, I don't know how to answer that exactly but yes, you could have made those choices, sure. Okay, what would have been in place is the uh, the knowledge that I could actually do it.

9. How did following a new vocational path impact those around you?

Julie: I show up excited, engaged, um, fun. I mean, we have fun here. We laugh every day. We work really hard. I probably do work harder here than I ever did before, but it's a good kind of hard work. Um, you know, you go home exhausted, but it's a good kind of exhausted. Um, not a drained feeling. They get more of me. Rather than it being pulled out of me or required by my corporate life. Um, it's voluntary. Um, I'll give everything I have because I believe in the cause and I'm not completely exhausted. I'm able to give more. And I think that translates to my direct reports, my team members, and ultimately our patients in our health center.

⬥

Sam: They, they see that I'm happier. And they're happier that I'm happier. And I'd show good – What I'm doing now, I'm much more, um, open about discussing, you know, who I am and what I'm doing. Rather than being a salesman, I just try to close the door at the end of the work day and not bring it home. Cause I, I couldn't do my – I mean, I wasn't – I mean, it's not, it was not work I could usually bring home.

⬥

Janet: Um, they can see my enthusiasm for sure. It sparks their interest because a lot of people think that – They stay in jobs that they hate, um, year after year after year because they, they get retirement. They get a, a check or they get benefits for life or whatever their reason is, and they're miserable. Um, and, and that's so sad. So now when I meet people, it's like they see my zest...I think, um, what goes on is that, um, I have a better relationship with myself and I'm happier —with myself. And, um, I'm relating – I relate with people in a different way. Yeah, so, um, I'm happier as, and I'm – I'm happier in my relationships, too, so it's easier to make friends — easier to listen to people.

❦

Riya: Uh, some went away as friends, and others, especially long-time friends, they just sort of watch in curiosity, and in – in a way, they know me – they've known me before I had any other career, so they just know that's Riya. She likes to explore. She does, you know – tons of people that know – knew me – my essential self. Uh, they – the people that knew me related around the company where I worked, for instance, I'm not in touch with most of those people. I attempted to stay in touch, but they just fell away, most of 'em. And then, um, then there's new – new people that have come, you know?

And family and friends love me, so – I have — no – nobody – no things – no waves created there, really. Uh, joy. I have joy and I have peace.

❦

Kyle: So I know in my, in my kids' heart, I'm better to be around.

I'm, I'm more of a father now. I mean, I was able to buy a car for my son yesterday.

⊷∾

Charlie: Well, I can – I can say in this moment, like right now, as I said, I'm really in a – in a – on a roll creatively and passionately, and I – I don't know if you saw them in pictures, but I dyed my beard bright blue.

And, um, it's very interesting because it gets so much attention and it allows me this opportunity to interact with people and, um, I am absolutely loving it. It's almost like a spiritual practice for me. It's like I have this attention, and I get to – I get to choose what I do with it in that moment, and it also – another thing that's really cool about it is that it makes me be on all the time when I'm not in public.

10. How did it impact your view of the world and your surrounding and others in your life?

Julie: I'm certainly able – I live and breathe with the sense of duty that I didn't have, um, before making this transition. Duty to serve, duty to fill all of these needs. Um, there's probably two dozen non-profit organizations that I want to be able to contribute to here in the Valley because now I see the need. I'm volunteering, my family's involved. Um, so I do see the need in a way that I didn't when I was kind of in that, you know, corporate hierarchy, you know, hamster wheel, traveling all over the place. I wasn't thinking of the social needs in my own backyard... I was all over the place, all over the country and international. So, being connected to this movement here in my own town, um, has certainly affected the way I see the economic and social issues, homelessness, hunger, healthcare education. Um, certainly changed that view for me.

⟨⟩

Sam: Um, I realized that truly, my only security is I – You know, economic security is creating multiple streams of income. And, um, you know, being true to myself and, and less fearful because I don't have to – You know, if one work opportunity, one consulting gig, whether I'm working as a part-time employee or as an independent contractor, um, falls apart. I, I won't be unemployed, I'll just be working part-time until I can find something else to fill in a gap. So I have more security overall. Overall, though, I'm

– Though my income once – Is not where it was. I mean, I had some problems. You know, did have bankrupt – I did lose my house. But you know, I'm still happier now that I'm renting and I'm starting over again financially.

⌘

Janet: Oh, wow. Um, I think it opened up possibilities. To – If I can do this, what, what other things can I do? You know, if I can do this for myself, can I use this same gift to volunteer or to donate a portion of my time to organizations, to non-profits, to maybe a inner-city non-profit that needs desperately some marketing material written or something like that? So, it kinda broadened my scope that way. I mean obviously, I mean there's – first of all, is that the world is – is the world of really ideas, right. And it's the world of ideas, and it's – there is recession of crisis, it's a recession of ideas and crisis, right.

⌘

Riya: Uh, it's – that makes me feel more relaxed in the world. It doesn't mean I'm apathetic, and it doesn't mean I don't work hard, and it doesn't mean I don't have an intention to maybe help improve something or change something, but I don't have anxiety around it. I – I have an acceptance of — um, all that is going on in the world, all the complexity, all the humanity, all – everything. And from there, it's a more powerful place to, uh, try to dream the next thing procreate with those.

⚜

Charlie: Um, I think that as I'm starting to write my bio lately is that I made this break with – with cultural reality. I took off and I left the United States, and I found out there's all these different ways to be and to do….

⚜

Ann: Um, yeah, it has in ways because one of the things when I was, you know, figuring out what it is that I wanted to do, you know, I sat down and worked on my goals. And one of my – you know, had very strong goals that I, you know, was very and still am, uh, but to a lesser degree, passionate about. Environmental and political issues and things like that. And – and I really, uh, felt that there was a disproportionate amount of, uh, distribution of wealth in the world. And so I really wanted to make an impact on those things. And so the old – older I get and the more estab-lished I get, of course, the more I, you know, see that I can make a difference in that.

And not just me though. I mean, the whole world is opening up to that, and I think it's wonderful. ...And so there's just so much opportunity here.

11. Can you describe if following a new vocational path had an impact on the relationships in your life and in which ways?

Julie: Um, sure. That's a deep question. I think – Well, the biggest would obviously be with my, with my spouse. Who really didn't get to see me those first few, you know, the first decade of our marriage, really. I – When you're home one weekend a month or, you know, a few days here or there. Um, we had a quite a long-distance relationship.

And so just being able to be home and have dinner together was really nice those, you know, the first few years after I made this transition.

Um, I've certainly gotten him involved in these social causes that I've, um, become more engaged in. Um, so it gives us opportunities to do things together. Um, my mom also lives here and she's a volunteer inside my organization now because, you know, that gets her some sense of support for me. Um, so that's changed the dynamic of that relationship as well. Those are the, the two big ones in my life.

Sam: Very positive also. My wife is a teacher.

And, um, and so she likes that we share it now. Also she kinda wishes I would shut up now. Where I was before, I wouldn't want to be talking about my day, and now I'm very open to talking about things. Um, uh, she's working on her doctorate. Um, and, and, uh, they're working on her EDD in, um, leadership. And has changed jobs, uh, and working down the hill as a, um, adult transition program for mild to moderate special ed high school seniors. And so she's gonna – And they're also kinda grooming her to become a, a program specialist to work outside the classroom more than, um, um, administrative. Supervisory job in that area, which is great. And my daughter, the boomerang, moved back home and, uh, at the end of college.

∾

Janet: You know, significant relationships, I guess if I, you know, ever have one or, you know, like a significant man/woman re-lationship, I think it would really affect it because even if they work, you know, in a full-time job, um, it still – You know, I would accept that. That's what their calling is. But it would affect me because I'm, I just want to be accepted for having a dif-ferent mindset.

Juan: Yeah, you know, I think yeah, absolutely, and this is something that I became more sensitive. Yeah, so I became more sensitive. I became more sensitive to myself, so I quit smoking, right. I think – I think, um, you know, especially my parents, I became so fond of them – I call them almost every two days, I'm calling them and – and feeling that love, you know. Uh-huh. That, um, I'm getting an emotion when I think about it 'cause — they are so great, great, great people. You know, and, um –I think yeah. I think we got – I got a little bit more feet on the ground.

⤜❧⤛

Riya: Yeah. Yeah, so the ones that were based on something, uh, I wanna say real, something — uh, beyond what you do and what – how you look and what you wear – those are – are strengthened and – probably immeasurably. Uh, and, um, and the other ones fall away. Anything that's superficial is — you know — not – not essential.

⤜❧⤛

Kyle: Um – I'm clear. I'm – I'm more clear. Okay, so I'm more clear. I think I'm more clear so people have said to me wow you – you've changed a lot — and really I hadn't changed, it's just that the, the, the stability of the vocation and the passion I had towards, towards my – the stability of uh, of the – of what I was doing and the passion I had for what I was doing allowed me to get rid of the, the um, the inhibited — I was not as inhibited. Um-hum, um-hum, um-hum...

I'm talking to my friends and we're talking and I'm really opening up and I know on Monday morning I'm gonna be happy because I'm going – you know – I'm going to be at work in my office doing my thing — and controlling my time –and – um, no inhibition so I can talk freely. I can be, you know, kind of clear.

❦

Charlie: Well, it's interesting, because right now, I'm – in the past year or two, I have sort of re- - I've gotten back into relationships with my family, my immediate family. Not my children family, but my mother and my siblings, and my sisters, uh, my sister, who is just a little bit older than me, is going through some health kind of related, mental health challenges, so I've been spending a lot of time with her, and my mother is in her 80s, and, um, she's doing really great, but she can use a hand once in a while, you know, so it's all – al of a sudden I'm involved with my family closer than I have been, um, and it's brought up a lot of compassion. It has developed, uh, working with my sister, and being with my sister has opened up this – this, uh, compassion. I mean, I could go into more details. I don't know how much you want to hear about that.

❧

Ann: Uh, yeah. It – it did. You know, um, there wasn't, um – there was, you know – there was some pressure. And it was a decision that I'd really kind of, uh, you know, had made on my own. I didn't, you know, really sit down and discuss it with my family or even my husband. Fortunately, he, you know, is good hearted and, you know, went along with, you know, what I wanted to do. But, um, so initially, you – you know, there – you know, maybe wasn't as smooth of a transition as I would have liked under different circumstances. Um, but now it's wonderful.

12. Can you tell me if following a new vocational path clarifies or highlights a greater purpose of your life?

Julie: Because this was about the same time, uh, within a year or so, when I decided it was time to start the doctoral program. And I have a quote on my wall, um, I didn't you know, "The purpose of life is a life of purpose." And that was the opening line of my Fielding dissertation because really, you know, what is the purpose of me being here? What is it that I'm to contribute to this planet?

⸎

Sam: Oh, yeah. Oh, definitely. It's one of those things that I had been pulled to do in, when I was in college by some wise people along the way. And so Joseph Campbell, Glen See and, and Bill Everson about, you know, getting quiet, getting quiet, listening for one's calling and then setting goals to achieve them. Achieve the calling, right, all that. And, and I, and I ignored that, uh, because of bad conditioning from my parents, which was, you know, make a living. And I think I had the wrong agenda and to get me out of the house at 18, you know? You know, and not having any money in the pot, you know? And so I, I was, you know, working in a much more fear-based, um, mode for decades. And now I don't have that. To the same degree, even though it might be more challenging one particular month to, you know, pay all the bills or whatever. I, I know that, that this is turning around nicely.

⸎

Janet: Um, I think like I said before, I think it's – The greater purpose is giving back and giving time, um, almost tithing a certain amount of time – So the big picture is that, is giving back and just giving of time, and my ultimate goal is to donate, um, a certain proceeds to either Trickle Up or one of the agent, one of those non-profits that take care of, like, third-world entrepreneurs. Like with basket weavers and different things, um, in third-world countries. So, and it's like donating, you know, a certain amount of money that helps them start their little business so they can feed their family.

❧

Juan: Uh, value something about me, um, that ceased a little bit to exist, and I started to have permission to have bigger dreams. Um, so I mean for me, my – my goal and my value right now is to – to have the roads alive… Yeah, exactly. So that's – that's a great sense of purpose that I have, and that is perfect for me because I can have all this emotional when it comes down to relating to people. And put it in action, you know, and having them relate with me, and see things for themselves.

❧

Kyle: Yeah, and, and you know what, it's actually boils down to helping people and being able to be a help in creating win-win situations for people which um, which I do in different angles.

Charlie: I think it has been refined. I think that, um, you know, uh, as a youngster, as a college person, I was interested in studying meditation and consciousness, and then I went off and I took this detour into dentistry and found some passion in cosmetic dentistry and learned a lot about a lot of things in that regard, and then that led me to getting out of dentistry and going on this big adventure. So I think of it all as a – it's all been – it's been, uh, following, it's been a path, and ... did that answer your question?

⌘

Anne: Well, yeah. I have real, you know – I mean, I have high ambitions. And you know, my personal agenda goal was to educate and empower as many people as I possibly could. And, I feel like I have, you know, done that. Uh, I – you know, I – I'd certainly make a bigger impact if I wanted to get out there and be more of a go getter, but I just don't want to do that at this point in my life. I think I started out with that much passion and enthusiasm, and now it's kind of like you know, it's just nice to just, you know, enjoy today.

13. How do you feel about yourself now that you made the change?

Julie: There, there is a pride in what I do. And it is a part of my identity now in a way that, um, I wouldn't have necessarily announced my company's name. If, you know, if we met at a, you know, at an event, I would've said, "Hi, I'm an HR leader." I wouldn't have told you the company I worked first. Right. The switch for me is I tell you now the company I work for first. "What do you do there?" "Oh, I do this and I do that." But, um, you know, this organization is actually part of my identity now. It's part of who I am.

❧

Sam: Oh, I feel better. I feel more genuine. It's like I, I don't have – Like when I was working and selling, maybe say going back to grad school days of being in retail and audio/video, I would feel sort of some conflict between myself in the workplace and myself off of work. And now I feel I'm the same person whether I'm –working or not.

❧

Janet: Um, I feel more confident, more self-confident than I ever have before.

Um, I feel more in control of my life because I am doing what I want to do. I can structure my business any way I want to do.

I am the boss, nobody's micromanaging me, I can microman-age myself if I want to. Um, so much more in control and more empowered. Much more personally empowered.

❧

Juan: Uh, well, I could see that the other path wasn't. [Laughs]. You know, the other of being morbid. Having a morbid life with no perspective. Just making money and then spending money, um, and watching porn wasn't really my, you know, my – my life. Like it's not a life that people can have. It's an option of life, but it's not the life that I can have or could have.

❧

Riya: Nothing to defend. I feel more settled with myself. Like there is nothing to prove. Um, felt really good about myself and that has a big part, that's a big thing to do with it.

❧

Charlie: Well, it's like – as I said before, right now in this mo-ment in my life, I'm just as excited to get up in the morning and excited to go to bed because of what I'm gonna dream about.

❧

Ann: Uh, I'm – I'm very pleased. I feel like I've, you know, made a – a, you know, a nice contribution and, uh, continue to do so. And, um, again, I like living a very relaxed, comfortable, uh, life and – and enjoying my family, my children, my community. Yeah. You know, whereas when I was younger and growing up, I was very ambitious. I always, uh, you know – here I had, you know, a full time business during the day, and I'd go to college full time at night and try to make straight A's and be on every committee, you know, and all that stuff. And, you know, that's a lot of pressure. But right now today, I want to enjoy today.

14. Can you tell me if following your new path altered either the priority or identification of what is most important to you?

Julie: Mm, definitely. Um, I think it's part of the change but it's also part of the life stage. Um, you know, caring and compassion. The ability to, you know, give of oneself.

Those are things that I don't think were on the surface for me before this transition.

⌘

Sam: Oh, yeah, definitely. Like what's really. And the answer is what everyone, you know, in the family has told me is, you know, it's the family, it's the caring, it's the, um, it's the being authentic in the moment. Being genuine in the moment.

❧

Janet: Um, I, I've always had, you know, since I come from the 50s, uh, I always had strong values as far as personal values, honesty and ethical and things like that. I have my business since 2008. I think it has showed me –   Shown me, um, ethical – That really importance of doing above and beyond what people expect, like the old business adage of, you know, over, um, over – Let's see. Under-deliver – Um, what's that? Over-promise.

❧

Juan: Let me put it different. Once, I saw that I was not okay, that the idea that I was not okay wasn't – wasn't real the focus on myself it started to decrease right, um, like this individual need to fix something about me or uh, value something about me, um, that ceased a little bit to exist, and I started to have permission to have bigger dreams. I think, again, it's probably not the essential values. It's whether or not I'm acting on them.

❧

Riya: As a priority every day. Or acting from them even, right?

Um, hmm – let me think about this one for a second. I always felt that I had pretty good value. I guess it – it tweaked them.

❧

Kyle: I guess you could say. Uh, it tweaked them, um, enlightened them so you –you get more enlightened — uh, with like the relationship with my family for example. Um-hum. Uh, you know that's a value that I had before but I couldn't do anything about it because I was miserable. So, even though I had the value, the value of, of, of having a good relationship with my children for example wasn't effective even though the value was there. So, it didn't change my value but it enlightened the value so now I can really act upon my values and I have more freedom to grow into my values. I think that's, I think that's the difference, enlightenment.

❧

Ann: Oh, did I change my values? Um, no. I don't really think I changed – well, I changed my values in that, yeah, you know, now I don't want as much of the stress or the pressure or the ambition or whatever. So – so that, yeah, as a value that now the value is more about, you know, um – you know, just living and enjoying, you know, today.

15. How do you measure or know that you made the right change for you?

Julie: You know, it's a nine out of 10, probably. Is it the perfect job for the rest of my life? No. There's obviously pluses and minuses of every job. But it, it hits just about every major box for me. So yeah, it was absolutely the right move. If I had it to do over again, I absolutely would have.

☙

Sam: Oh, well, it's, it's one of those things that waking up in the morning and not dreading going to work. I can kinda measure my emotional state. Uh, you know, I know what I'm doing by going to Outlook because of having multiple tutoring clients and, and, you know, class – Classes different days of – My classes different days of the week and, um, balancing that with my online teaching. I make my own schedule. I am not reporting to a, a boss 40 hours a week, and that is a great sense of freedom.

☙

Janet: How do I know? Because first, because of the fulfilled feeling. It's like you just know inner, in your inner self. Right. It's an emotion. It's, um, it's an inner sense of fulfillment.

Riya: Honestly, it's how I feel inside, you know, every day. Yeah, it's not there's no external, quantitative – the – the thing is the external follows, for sure. Um, you know, the – job I have – the jobs I have now, they're more fulfilling. They have more flexibility. I'm rewarded more for more creativity and deep thinking.

Um, and I get paid more.

❧

Kyle: Um, I think I'm, I, I, I've – I measure it by, uh, the passion I think that I have.

Uh, I measure it by – and I never sat and thought well how do I measure this…

I guess to answer your question and I'm going around and about but I guess it's the passion.

❧

Ann: Because, um, by the way I feel. And you know, the wonderful relationship that I have with, uh, you know, my husband. We've been married 30 years and our children. And, um, yeah. And with my friends and family. So much more relaxed and, you know, definitely it's better.

16. Has your financial situation been effected since you made the change?

Sam: Overall, though, I'm – Though my income once – Is not where it was. I mean, I had some problems. You know, did have bankrupt – I did lose my house. But you know, I'm still happier now that I'm renting and I'm starting over again financially.

⌘

Janet: But I would say those are the main ones. Money – Financially, um, just worrying about chasing – You know, you're always chasing, um, to, to make what you need to live on. That, that can be an obstacle. But it can also motivate you, too.

⌘

Juan: Uh, that was tough. That was tough. That was really tough. [Laughs]. So first of all, I really, um, I did things without a great planning to be honest with you. 'Cause I was so fed up. I think. I remember living so out of sync in –authenticity, but, um, yeah, so I was – I was unemployed for almost one year, and then I worked with this firm making $24,000 a year. From almost $180,000 a year to $24,000 a year. That's a huge gap. And, um, but I managed to live, and I wasn't really unhappy, but, um, it was a little stressful because having to live with these concerns of money and then concerns for the future –how things are gonna look like. Um, so it was really tough, and – and I had to return my car and I was driving a Volvo 99. And it was terrible problems. And I was living in Florida and it was tough to get a job there. I didn't wanna work back in and etc. So but you know, things at the end worked out. And then I came to San Francisco and I – I'm working as a consultant. And overall, I get paid more than I did before.

⸎

Riya: I had to take – you know, know that definitely the place where I took a risk and – and incurred some debt to get training and – and coaching and all that, but that – that's almost done now. So I'm in a better a – you know, a better place for the long term. Yeah, and I don't – I don't worry about – I don't count my change for, you know, food and things like that – groceries. Which I was doing [giggles]. It was very, uh –Yeah. – tight budget for a little while there. Uh, it's uh, 100 percent turn around.

Kyle: There's no issues with money anymore. [laughs] I, I, I just — pay the –Money. Yeah, I mean I just bought my son a car yesterday — and that was really – well, you know, I'm gonna have him make payments on it because I'm trying to teach him responsibility — but at least I was able to go it's a used car but it's able to go — we'll just pay cash for the car — and, and I picked him up at school and it was all because of the vocation. You know? I was able to pick him up early at school he didn't know I was coming. And it all goes back to the vocation. You know? So that little thing right there and it's – it's a big thing really. I could've never done that before. Knowing that – I mean I – I didn't even think about it till last night and I reflected on oh my God, I bought my son a car — went and picked him up at his – oh my God — like I got overwhelmed a little bit last night like what did I just do, I didn't even know, I didn't even realize – that it was making me feel so good at that time. You know I didn't even need – I didn't need to dawn on it because it's just – it's just second nature now. So, that's what it's enabled me to do just to have that freedom.

❧

Charlie: Well, I made – I had a pretty big windfall, um, when I left dentistry. As I mentioned, I ended up selling major assets, some of them that I didn't even know I had, and I had a huge, um, financial cushion, shall I say, and, um, so I had this incredible freedom that I had never even – was beyond my wildest dreams to have that much money. Um, and so it was – that was

what an amazing experience to have, and, um, and somehow

I thought it was going to last forever, and, um, eventually the

money started to run out. It certainly got less and less, and I got

to a point where I actually, um, I actually gave my house back to

the bank. I ended up moving in with my mom, which turned

out to be a pretty good situation in the long run. And the money

is showing up, and the people are showing up, and it's happening

on a shoestring, and it's really, really happening. Yes, and they're

– and the cash flow – you know, it's like the money shows up or

somebody shows up when I need it.

∽∾

Ann: Well, yeah. It's been affected. And so now, of course, once

we got going, you know, it was certainly a lot better. A lot better.

17. Has your diet, exercise and rest been affected since the change?

Julie: You know, it was better probably at the beginning. Um,

you know, so right after the change, the first couple of years,

much, much better. So that was kind of de-stressing, kind of,

you know, um, detoxing. From all those years. Um, it's probably,

you know, from a diet and health and exercise, um – I'm not too terribly far away from where I was, um, when I first left corporate America.

◈

Sam: Not so much. I'm – I have changed doctors – My diet's fine. Uh, sleep's never been a problem. I, you know, I had, you know – Actually, I guess I have taken better care of my health because I was diagnosed with sleep apnea, and I'm getting help with that – My wife is only concerned about the snoring, but, um –Getting, getting to help me breathe at night. Other than – It's never been much of a problem.

◈

Janet: Yes, for the positive. Because I was working out before, I was – And you know I, I was weight training and exercising and, and I am very, very healthy eater. So it has only taken that to the next level. And if you have discipline, which you need self-discipline if you're gonna run a business. If you're not self-disciplined in, um, it's gonna be really hard to maintain the structure of a, any kind of business.

But diet, exercise, um, you know go to church, things like that. It's, it's all gonna be impacted for the better. Sleep? Um, being a mid-lifer, you know, most, most nights it's okay, but some nights – I don't stay up worrying about, you know, money or anything like that. I just, um, some nights you're just not gonna – You're, you're too wound up. And I like to read, like, personal development books right before I go to bed. And sometimes you need to keep a pad and pencil right before your, - right by your bedside, um, and jot down those ideas that are coming to you right before you go to sleep.

&

Juan: Yeah, well, I think, um, the first thing I did was that I quit smoking and never came back again. So, um, it was, uh, some work that I – I had to do with myself with — releasing some emotions, you know, clearing up some things that weren't very clear in my life, and just living the way, clearing the path. Um, and, you know, with that, you know, opened up the, you know, the whole thing of taking care of myself, you know. Um, so I'm exercising every day. Right. Um, my plan is to – I still have to lose a lot.

&

Riya: The main one is sleep. I've always sort of had a good diet and exercise – routine, but the – the main is sleep, and, um, I think with the reduction in – in anxiety – anxiety. I don't – I'm not a super anxious person, but I can feel when I'm alert and sort of that cortisol is running. Um-hum. Um-hum. You know – 'cause you're a little stressed, that low-level stress that you have on all the time, that – that goes off now. And, uh, my – my sleep is – I've – I've always tried to, also, sleep eight hours or sleep that all I need, but, um, when you can – when you have a little more flexibility and you can sleep to the actual rhythm of the day — uh, that's even better. So I – I think that's – it's a much healthier place to be, and I wish it – it would be available for everybody.

❧

Kyle: That's a great question because you know what, my diet and exercise was good before –but it –it also it was under stress before. So, I had a good diet and I had good exercise but it was forced. I had to force it. So, it was good before but after – you know – I got some secure and freedom now it's like my diet and exercise is easy. So it's – I mean it's like it flows better. My body flows better. So, I'm in, you know, I – I can do better. As far as sleep goes it's, it's – it's night and day. I mean I get to sleep like a rock.

❧

Charlie: Oh, much better. I mean, I'm like, I – I have more energy now than – than I've ever had in my life.

18. What are you doing now to further develop yourself?

Julie: Complete a non-profit leadership certification. Um, the – Obviously the doctoral work. You know, I see myself, you know, the next kind of phase is taking my experience here and being able to leverage that and share that with other organizations. So post-doc, I would see, you know, consulting and partnering with other organizations.

⟡

Sam: I'm always looking for the, looking for some new thing. Trying to build this, trying to build that. You know, keeping the working going on. Even if I'm, you know, booked 100 percent, you never know what's gonna come on down the pike, so always looking for those opportunities.

⟡

Juan: I'm taking a class right now that my company's paying for a PMP certification, so in April, I'm gonna do a test to be a project manager professional. So it's like a CPA. And, um, and then I'm taking the risk management cert, uh, professional. Um, which is, uh, you know, another certification for this work. And I'm work-

ing for my papers for my my third college, which is the – not
MFA, but MBA.

***

Riya: I think – I actually have been doing teacher training. I've
sort of been mentored as a teacher. Well, uh, it's for the healing arts –I've been doing that. – um, I may go to law school.
[Laughs]. Yes. Well, I'm interested – I mean, right now, I am
already sort of in the intellectual property world, but I have an
interest in environmental law –which I think goes well with technology. And then I got encouragement from the attorneys at the
firm. And so, you know, we'll see. I'm gonna – We'll see. Yeah.
[Laughs].

***

Kyle: I do an hour everyday of continuing education –uh, and
I use, I use mainly the mentors –and teachers that, that um, that
sell materials –and I'm also connected with a group out of southern Cal that um, we network with and we, and we uh – they have
uh, a web based site – – with all kinds of educational learning
and stuff on it so I put in about – now I can put in about an hour
a day. When I first started I was putting in six hours a day –of

education.. Now I've gotten to a point where I hear a lot of the same old things over and over and over but then I find the nugget — of the new things and then there's updated things. Uh, so – Um-hum. The point I'm making is that — you only – what, what happens is and it goes back to what I said earlier is that the tools will be there when you go. If you just go and you take a step forward the tools will be there. Well, the hour education a day it brings in more tools. So, I do it yes I do it to open up — open up more – more imagination.

⊱⊰

Charlie: I'm doing Kundalini yoga right now three or four times a week with a class, with a, you know, with an instructor, and then almost every morning I do a little bit of it, and I think that – that entails a lot of, uh, for me, it's like meditation. It's chanting, it's physical, it's brass, it's energy, it's ... and, um, and that allows me to keep the channel open, and, um, I mean, it seems like every morning I – I get some kind of a download that's like, "Oh, my God. Oh, my God, where did that come from?" You know, like, a project, and I – an aspect of two projects or three projects comes to-gether to form something that I didn't even imagine would – would come my way, and clear my path, or smooth – put wind in my sail.

Ann: Um, you know, I try to keep up with, you know, the businesses that I'm in and kind of, you know, see what's out there. So I do get online enough that I can, you know, pay attention to what else is going on. But I don't do, you know – again, I don't worry too much about that. I'm – I live in the moment. And, um, you know, that's what makes me feel good or happy, you know, for now. And I trust that all is – all is well. And all will be well.

19. What are the current challenges if you have any in your life?

Julie: Um, there's a level of, um, there is, there is a level of challenge in terms of how committed I am to the organization. Um, boy. That I haven't set as strong of boundaries that I used to in corporate America. Um, and let my work – Because it so much a part of me, let it kind of, um, trickle over. Kind of spill over. Um –There have been times where it's been a negative. Um – Well, I guess, I guess kind of a tactical example is as a corporate HR person, I knew that I was in the role of an HR person, and I never allowed friendships or relationships with my workmates to cross anything more than a "Let's go have lunch during work" event. In this environment, we really are a pretty strong family, so there are very few boundaries. Um, we're at each other's house, we're involved in each other's family. But, um, it's, it's been one of the larger challenges for me because I've let those walls down, and now had to figure out where that right boundary is. And there's some pain with that when you, you kind of give more than you really should have. Um, I've let myself get taken advantage of. You know, I've, I've put the organization first over maybe family members or other relationships.

∞

Sam: You know, it's, it's, it's an ongoing process for me to look for new opportunities and, and keep it going. And that, that's where, you know, my sense of security comes in. That I know that oh yeah, I can make a change and I can look several months in the future rather than wondering whether or not my office is going to close or I'm gonna get laid off or have a commission cut or something like that, which is what I was living with for many, many years before this. Yeah, so now this is under your own control. It's under my own control, and we all have to make those adjustments. I, I think – I'm, I'm – I may just be front – I have to plan it to make those – I won't speak for anybody else, but I have to make those adjustments to myself. As changes in my circumstances come up. And if they're outside of my control, I can adjust it, but it's not a life-or-death, fight-or-flight type of –Big thing. I'm,

I'm teaching my immune sys – I, I mean my, uh, um, nervous system to calm down when the unexpected bill comes in or, um, an opportunity dries up. I can, I can go and find myself in that by looking into the future and taking action towards that.

❧

Janet: The challenges come from, uh, self, self-confidence. Sometimes you get clients that no matter – It's not you, it's they're not gonna be happy no matter what. But it – For me, it shakes my self-confidence. Um, I did a, a project. A, a series of baseball articles for a person, and they had paid, you know, a very small amount before. Wasn't happy. You know, I charged him twice as much. Uh, he wasn't happy. I redid all of them, took me a ton of time. He wasn't happy. Um, some clients just aren't gonna be happy. So, so, you know, issues with self-confidence. You know, it did kinda shake that. Um – Levels of doubt as far as am, am I good enough? You know, that imposter syndrome of they're gonna find out that I only have a high-school diploma and that I really don't know what I'm talking about or what I'm doing, and they're gonna find somebody more qualified. And self-doubt, things like that. That's been obstacles. But I would say those are the main ones. Money – Financially, um, just worrying about chasing – You know, you're always chasing, um, to, to make what you need to live on. That, that can be an obstacle. But it can also motivate you, too.

∞

Riya: You have to prioritize – make choices. Um, that's – that's really the challenge is to not put too many things on my plate in a day or a week – – and know that I can shut that down, and then I'll come back to it 'cause there's just, um, you know, an abundance of things, and that's great. I just have to juggle 'em – Uh, current challenges are – well, there's always challenges. Uh, so my current challenges is uh, buying properties at, at the right – at the prices that we need to buy them out.

∞

Kyle: Uh, we get them uh, but they trickle in, they trickle in slow, it's not really selling them anymore, — it's not really, if we're holding the property it, it's not really filling the properties anymore either, it's – our challenge now is, because of market has turned – – and everybody's coming out of the woodworks now so I've got a –

– lot of competition in buying the right properties uh, and a, and a lot of people don't know what they're doing and they come in and they, you know, they make a lot of mistakes at everybody's expense. So, you know, if it was all real professionals and we do – there is a few of us out there – wouldn't be a problem but uh, that's probably my biggest challenge along with um, the slow process of getting the right people in the right place, in the right seat.

❧

Charlie: Um, you know, I don't know. Maybe a couple of months ago I might have said financial challenges, but it's not. It's – it's hard for me to, um, it's hard for me to even focus on something being a challenge. It's just – it's just, um, what am I going to do and how am I going to find a way to do it? It's like everything's a challenge. Life is – from some perspectives, life is just problems. You know? If you want to look at it that way. Or life is a game, and you're just taking steps, clearing the – clearing the problems out of the way by focusing your awareness on them and letting them operate in front of you so you can take the next step into that space. Yeah, so I mean – and even challenges to me is like – I don't even – it's like, it's a – to me, rephrasing or finding another way for a - challenge is too negative to me, you know what I mean? Challenges don't even fit for me. It's just like, adventure.

20. Where do you see yourself in 5 years?

Julie: Um, Ph.D. And contributing, um, you know, in a similar way but to more organizations. Sharing these gifts and this experience with more – Sort of what I'm giving, I'm giving now to just one organization. I would see being able to help multiple organizations. Um, just what I – I jotted down a few things to trigger my memory because it's been, it's been a while since I made this transition. Um, the one thing that was really clear for me was, um, I really had to step completely away from everything when I made this transition. . So there was this cleansing detox, you know, stripping away of the old identity. And then over the last few years, rebuilding that to create kind of this new persona, as you, as you put it. This new professional identity. And now I say without hesitation, I hardly ever tell everybody what I used to do.

❧

Janet: Um, I would like my business to be completely referral based. I would just like to say, "I only take two projects a month." I would like the freedom to be able to say, "This – I'm not taking any new clients right now. There's a waiting list."

Uh, marketing projects. I do a lot of website content.

Riya: Hmm, now that's a good question because I've done a lot of goal setting, a lot of goal work and I used to uh, um, try to set, you know,] goals month, uh, day by day, month by month and –

❦

Kyle: I try to –project exactly what I wanted five years from now or whatever – and shoot for that but as time went on, my goals have changed – Um-hum. – in the things that I wanna have changed. So, I started kind of backing up on how I envision myself in five years from now, lightly because I really don't really care that much. I really don't care that much about having all this stuff. For example, I'm totally okay where I'm at right now in the, in the place – in the house that I live in now, I'm fine with it. The car that I drive now, I'm fine with it. Um, but I envision myself having a 3,000 square foot home overlooking the mountains over here in the foothills and having a place in SoCal and driving a new SUV and great relationships with my children. I always envisioned myself working from my laptop and having my business organized.

❦

Ann: Well, yeah. I have real, you know – I mean, I have high ambitions. And you know – you know, my personal agenda goal was to educate and empower as many people as I possibly could. And I feel like I have, you know, done that. Uh, I – you know, I – I'd certainly make a bigger impact if I wanted to get out there and be more of a go getter, but I just don't want to do that at this point in my life. I think I started out with that much passion and enthusiasm, and now it's kind of like you know, it's just nice to just, you know, enjoy today.

21. What advice would you give to someone today who is between 40 and 55 on what steps to take to find a better alignment with their own work?

Julie: You gotta listen to that voice. That voice knows. That voice knows.

❧

Sam: There's maybe trial and errors and don't give up ... – I've had to make some, numerous changes heading me towards that direction and, and the tutoring helps teach jobs.

❧

Janet: Do a lot of research on that subject. Check out your competition, see what other people – And that's the first thing I did was I saw, um, you know, I went online, found out what other people are charging, what other people are doing, what their styles are. Everybody offers something a little bit different. Everybody, you know, uh, do your research. Check out your competition. Um, you know, try – Give some things away. . Establish in social media, um, to establish yourself as an expert. Put yourself out there, um, you know, give little tips. And that's what I did on LinkedIn.

⁂

Juan: Well, first of all, see why you got yourself into it, right. Don't blame yourself, right. Don't try to change anything with yourself because there's nothing wrong with yourself. All the ideas that you had of – of yourself or of something wrong with you was not true. Then when you see that, you have the freedom to now go after of what you really like to do. And what you were made for. Well, I know that's going to be hard to quit your job because of the security there so you're gonna have to put in extra time to do what I just said.

⁂

Kyle: First of all, find the people that are doing what you want to do. So, if you have – first of all you need to figure out what you wanna do. So, I guess we're assuming that you kind of know what you wanna do but you can't do it. So, what you want to do is at any spare time, anytime that you have you need to re-search the people that are already doing it because in almost every vocation out there are a lot of teachers and a lot of mentors for specialized learning. You need to get specialized learning – – and I would recommend you go and say I'm gonna go back to college because I wanna be so and so or whatever unless you're trying to be a doctor or a lawyer.

⚬≈⚬

Ann: Oh, I just highly encourage them, highly encourage them to pursue it at whatever level that they're comfortable in doing. I know everybody's situation is different. You know, you can't just up and quit your job or do something different. Or if you've already got a very, um, busy life, and sometimes it's really hard to incorporate, you know, adding something else to your sched-ule. But I just think it is really important, and I think it's, um, for people, you know, just health wise and, you know, happi-ness, everything to find something that you are passionate about and go with the pace that feels comfortable for you because you don't want added stress on yourself or your family situation. But definitely start heading in the direction of where your passion is and, um – and in the, you know, uh – the money does usually follow, you know. You've also got to, of course, figure out how you're going to, you know, create your livelihood in your passion. But when you're so – you're doing something that you absolutely love to do and you're passionate about it, it's a lot easier to make money with it. And you know, if you are having to work harder, long hours, at least you're so much happier because you're doing what you love. You know, staying in a job that you – that you really don't like, uh, you know, for longer than necessary is bad for your health.

⊷❧

Charlie: Figure out what makes you happy and just do that. Uh-huh. Simple, but very precise advice. Yeah.

References

Adler, A. (1964). The individual psychology of Alfred Adler: A systematic
presentation in selections from his writings. New York, NY:
Harper & Row.

Alighieri, D. (1996). The divine comedy. Oxford, England:
Oxford University Press.

Allport, G.W. Vernon, P.E., & Lindsey, G. (1960). A study of values.
Boston, MA: Mifflin.

American Association of Retired People. (n.d).
Retrieved from http://www.aarp.org

Ansbacher, H.L., & Ansbacher, R.R. (1956). The individual psychology
of Alfred Adler. New York, NY: Harper & Row.

Bandura, A. (1980). Gauging the relationship between self-efficacy
judgment and action. Cognitive Therapy and
Research, 4, 263-268.

Bardwick, J. (1986). The plateauing trap. New York, NY: Bantam.

Bateson, C. (2010). Composing a further life.
New York, NY: Alfred A. Knopf.

Bateson, G. (1972). Steps to an ecology of mind.
New York, NY: Ballantine Books.

Baumeister, R.F. (1991). Meanings of life.

New York, NY: The Guilford press.

Becker, E. (1971). Birth and death of meaning.

New York, NY: Free Press.

Becker, E. (1973). The denial of death.

New York, NY: Free Press.

Bell, D. (1956). Work and its discontents. The cult of Efficiency in

America. Boston, MA: Beacon Press.

Boldt, L. (1996). How to find the work you love. New York, NY: Arkana.

Borysenko, J. (2011). Fried: Why you burn out and how to revive.

New York, NY: Hay House.

Brammer, L., & Abrego, P. (1981). Interventions strategies for coping

with transitions. The Counseling Psychologist, 9, 19-36.

Brehony, K. (1996). Awakening at midlife.

New York, NY: Riverhead Press.

Brewer, J. (1922). National Vocational Guidance Bulletin.

Journal of Counseling and Development, 1(4), 1-24.

Brown, D. (2002). The role of work and cultural values in occupational

choice, satisfaction, and success: A theoretical statement. Journal

of Counseling and Development,. 80(1), 48-56.

Brown, S. D. & Lent, R. W. (2008). Social cognitive career theory and subjective well-being in the context of work. Journal of Career Assessment, 16(1), 6-21. doi: 10.1177/1069072707305769

Browning, D. (2007). Slow love: How I lost my job, put on my pajamas, and found happiness. New York, NY: Atlas.

Campbell, J. (1968). The hero with a thousand faces. Princeton, NJ: Princeton University Press.

Carstensen, L. (2009). A long bright future: An action plan for a lifetime of happiness, health, and financial security. New York, NY: Broadway Books.

Carter, A. (1995). Mahatma Gandhi: A selected bibliography (Bibliographies of world leaders). Westport, CT: Greenwood Press.

Chalofsky, N. (2010). Meaningful workplaces: Reframing how and where we work. San Francisco, CA: Jossey-Bass.

Chope, R. C. (2006). Introduction to the special issue on social justice and career development. Career Planning and Adult Development Journal, 21, 3–9.

Chope, R. C. (2011). Reconsidering interests: The next big idea in career counseling theory and research. Journal of Career Assessment, 19, 343.

Cochran, L. (1990). The sense of vocation: A study of career and life development. Albany State University of New York.

Corbett, D. (2006). Portfolio life: The new path to work, purpose, and passion after 50. San Francisco, CA: Jossey-Bass.

Csikszentmihalyi, M. (1975). Beyond boredom and anxiety. San Francisco, CA: Jossey-Bass.

Csikszentmihalyi, M. (1988). Optimal experience. New psychological studies of flow in consciousness. New York, NY: Cambridge University Press.

Csikszentmihalyi, M. (1990). Flow. New York, NY: Harper & Row.

Csikszentmihalyi, M. (1997). Finding flow. New York, NY: Basic Books.

Davidman, L. (2000). Motherloss. Berkely: University of California Press.

Deci, E. (1975). Intrinsic motivation. New York, NY: Plenum Press.

Department of Health and Human Services. (2011). Administration on aging. Retrieved from http://www.aoa.gov/aoaroot/aging_statistics/index.aspx

Dewey, J. (1933). How we think: A restatement of the relation of reflective thinking to the educative process (Revised ed.). Boston, MA: D. C. Heath.

Dychtwald, K., & Kadlec, D. J. (2009). With purpose: Going from success to significance in work and life. New York, NY: Collins Living.

Edwards, C.L. (2008). Midlife crisis. International encyclopedia of the social sciences. Retrieved from http://www.encyclopedia.com/doc/1G2-3045301550.html

Emslie, C. & Hunt, K. (2009). "Live to work" or "Work to live"? A qualitative study of gender and work–life balance among men and women in mid-life. Gender, Work, & Organization, 16(1), 151-172. DOI: 10.1111/j.1468-0432.2008.00434

Erikson, E. (1959). Identify and the lifecycle. Psychological Issues Monographs, 1(1), 1-171.

Erikson, E. (1986). Identity, youth and crisis. New York, NY: Norton.

Evans, P., & Bartolome, F. (1981). Must success cost so much? New York, NY: Basic Books.

Evans, P., & Bartolome, F. (1986). The dynamics work family: Relationships in managerial lives. Journal of Applied Psychology, 35(3), 371-395.

Fiske, M.L. (1980). Changing hierarchies of commitment in adulthood. Cambridge, MA: Harvard University Press.

Frankl, V. (1984). Man's search for meaning. New York, NY: Simon & Schuster.

Freedman, M. (2011). The big shift. New York, NY: Perseus Books.

Freud, S. (1914). Psychopathology of everyday life. New York, NY: Macmillan.

Fromm, E. (1941). Escape from freedom. New York, NY: Henry Holt.

Fromm, E. (1994). On being human. New York, NY: Continuum.

Garfinkel, P. (2006). Buddha or bust: In search of truth, meaning, happiness, and the man who found them all. New York, NY: All Crown.

Goldman, C. (2009). Who am I now that I am not who I was? Conversations with women in midlife and the years beyond. Cambridge, MA: Nodin Press.

Gottfredson, L. S. (1982). Vocational research priorities. The Counseling Psychologist, 10(2), 69-84.

Gould, R.L. (1972). The phases of adult life. American Journal of Psychiatry, 129, 521-531.

Halberstam, J. (2000). Work. New York, NY: Berkeley Press.

Hall, D.T., & Rabinowitz, S. (2008). Maintaining employee involvement in a plateaued career. The International Journal of Human Resource Management, 19(4), 582-599.

Handy, C. (1991). The age of unreason. Boston, MA: Harvard Business Review Press.

Handy, C. (1999). Waiting for the mountain to move. San Francisco, CA: Jossey-Bass.

Heppner, P. P., & Krauskopf, C. J. (1987). An information-processing approach to personal problem solving. The Counseling Psychologist, 15, 371-447.

Herzberg, F. (1966). Work and the nature of man. New York, NY: The New American library.

Holland, J.L. (1997). Making vocational choices: A theory of vocational personalities and environments. Odessa, FL: Psychological Assessment.

Hollis, J. (2001). Creating a life: Finding your individual path. Toronto, ON: Inner City Books.

Hollis, J. (2003). On this journey we call our life: Living the questions. Toronto, ON: Inner City Books.

Hollis, J. (2006). Finding meaning in the second half of life: How to finally really grow up. New York, NY: Gotham Books.

Hudson, F. (1995). Lifelaunch. Santa Barbara, CA: Hudson Institute Press.

Ibrahim, F.A. Ohnishi, H. & Wilson, R.P. (1994). Career assessment in a culturally diverse society. Journal of Career Assessment, 2, 276-288.

Jaffe, A. (1984). Myth of meaning: Work of C. Jung. Zurich, Switzerland: Daimon.

James, W. (1955). The principles of psychology. Mineola, NY: Dover.

Jung, C. (1954). The development of personality. Princeton, NJ: Princeton University Press.

Jung, C. (1957). The Undiscovered Self. New York, NY: A Mentor Book.

Jung, C. (1959). Aion. Princeton, NJ: Princeton University Press.

Krishnamurti, J. (1987). Awakening of intelligence. New York, NY: HarperCollins.

Lambley, P. (1995). The middle-aged rebel. Rockport, MA: Element Books.

Langer, E. (1997). Mindfulness. Reading, MA: Addison-Wesley.

Lawrence-Lightfoot, S. (2009). The third Chapter: Passion, risk, and adventure in the 25 years after 50. New York, NY: Farrar, Strauss, & Giroux.

Leider, R., & Shapiro, D. (2004). Claiming your place at the fire. San Francisco, CA: BK Books.

Lent, R.W., & Brown, S.D. (2011). Social cognitive approach to career development. The Career Development Quarterly 44(4), 310-321. DOI: 10.1002/j.2161-0045.1996.tb00448

Leshan, E. (1973). The wonderful crisis of middle age. New York, NY: Warner Books.

Levinson, D. (1978). The seasons of a man's life. New York, NY: Ballantine Books.

Levoy, G. (1997). Callings: Finding and following an authentic life. New York, NY: Harmony Books.

Lewin, K. (1935). A dynamic theory of personality. New York, NY: McGraw-Hill.

Luther, M. (1913). Luther's correspondence and other contemporary letters. Philadelphia, PA: The Lutheran Publication Society.

McAdams, D. P. (1993). The stories We Live By. New York, NY: Guilford Publications.

MacArthur Foundation. (2012). National Institute on aging, University of Wisconsin. Retrieved from http://www.agingsocietynetwork.org/

Marx, K. (1963). Karl Marx: Early writings. (T.B. Bottomore, Ed. & Trans) New York, NY: McGraw-Hill.

Matheson, P.E. (1916). The discourses of Epictetus. Oxford, England: The Clarendon Press.

May, R. (1973). Man's search for himself. New York, NY: Dell.

Mayer, N. (1978). The male mid-life crisis. Oxford, England: Doubleday.

McAdams, D.P., Josselson, R., & Lieblich, A. (2006). Identity and story. Creating self in narrative. Washington, DC: American Psychological Association.

Meneuhin, Y. (1978). Unfinished journey. London, England: Futura.

Miller, D. C., & Form, W. H. (1951). Industrial sociology. New York, NY: Harper.

Mitchell, L.K., & Krumboltz, J.D. (1996). Krumboltz's learning theory of career choice and counseling. In D. Brown, L. Brooks, & Associates (Eds.) Career choice and development (3rd ed.) San Francisco, CA: Jossey Bass.

Moore, T. (1992). Care of the soul. New York, NY: HarperCollins.

Morin, A. (1995). Characteristics of an effective internal dialogue in the acquisition of self-information. Imagination, Cognition, and Personality, 15(1). 45-58.

Motulsky, S. L. (2010). Relational processes in career transition: Extending theory, research, and practice. The Counseling Psychologist, 38, 1078-1114. doi:10.1 177/0011000010376415

MOW International Research Team. (1987). The meaning of working. London, England: Academic Press.

Neugarten, B. (1968). Age norms, age constraints and adult socialization. Chicago, IL: University of Chicago Press.

Norton, D. L. (1976). Personal destinies: A philosophy of ethical individualism. Princeton University Press.

Ochberg, R. (1987). Middle-aged sons and the meaning of work. Ann Arbor, MI: UMI Research Press.

Osipow, S.H. (1969). What do we really know about career counseling? National Conference on Guidance and Placement, Columbia: University of Missouri.

Palmer, M. (2007). The book of Chuang Tzu. New York, NY: Penguin.

Parsons, F. (1909). Choosing a vocation. Boston, MA: Houghton Mifflin.

Patterson, D. G., & Darley, J. G. (1936). Men, women, and jobs. University of Minnesota Press.

Patton, W., & McMahon, M. (2006). Career development and systems theory. Rotterdam, Netherlands: Sense Publishers.

Pepper, S.C. (1942). World hypotheses: A study in evidence. Berkeley University of California Press.

Pinder, C. C. (1984). Work motivation. Glenview, IL: Scott, Foresman.

Raines, H. (1994). Fly fishing through the mid-life crisis. Harpswell, ME: Howell Anchor Books.

Reid, J. D., & Willis, S. L. (1999). Middle age: New thoughts, new directions. In S. L. Willis & J. D. Reid (Eds.), Life in the middle: Psychological and social development in middle age. (p. 277).San Diego, CA: Academic Press.

Reisman, D. (1961). The lonely crowd. New Haven, CT: University Press.

Roach, M. (2011). And I shall have some peace there. New York, NY: Grand Central.

Robin, C. (1998). Existential perspectives on meaningful work. Santa Barbara, CA: The Fielding Institute Press.

Rodgers, C. (1961). On becoming a person: A therapist's view of psychotherapy. Boston, MA: Houghton Mifflin.

Roe, A. (1956). The psychology of occupations. New York, NY: Wiley.

Rounds, J.B. (1990). The comparative and combined utility of work value and interest data in career counseling with adults. Journal of Vocational Behavior, 37(1), 37-45.

Sarason, S. (1977). Work, aging, & social change. Shepherdstown, WV: Pavillion IV Books.

Scott, D., & Jaffe, D. (2004). Managing personal change. Dallas, TX: Axzo Press.

Sheehy, G. (1995). New passages. New York: NY: Merritt Corporation.

Shoffner Creager , M.F. (2011). Practice and research in career counseling and development. The Career Development Quarterly, 59(6), 482-527.

Sievers, B. (1986). Beyond the surrogate of motivation. Organizational Studies, 7(4), 335-351.

Sinetar, M. (1987). The actualized worker. The Futurist (EUA), 21(2), 21-25.

Steinem, G. (2006). Doing sixty and seventy. San Francisco, CA: Elders Academy Press.

Super, D. E. (1953). A theory of vocational development. American Psychologist, 8, 185–190.

Super, D. E. (1990). A life-span, life-space approach to career development. In D. Brown, L. Brooks, & Associates (Ed.), Career choice and development. San Francisco, CA: Jossey-Bass Publishing.

Swenson, D. (2000). Something about Kierkegaard. Macon, GA: Mercer University Press.

Tamir, L.M. (1989). Modern myths about men at midlife: An assessment. In S. Hunter, & M. (Sundel, Eds.), Midlife myths: Issues, findings and practice implications (pp.157-180). Newbury Park, CA: Sage.

Taylor, F. (1911). Principles of scientific management. New York, NY: Harper & Brothers.

Terkel, S. (1975). Working. New York, NY: Avon.

Tiedeman, D., & O'Hara, R. (1963). Career development: Choice and adjustment. New York, NY: College Entrance Examination Board.

Toms, M., and Toms, J. (1998). True work. New York, NY: Bell Tower.

Tracey, T. J. G. (2007). Moderators of the interest congruence-occupational outcome relation. International Journal for Educational and Vocational Guidance, 7, 37–45.

Underhill, E. (2003). The cloud of unknowing: The classic of medieval mysticism. New York, NY: Dover.

United States Census Bureau: (2012). Life expectancy by sex, age, and race. Retrieved from http://www.census.gov/compendia/statab/cats/births_deaths_marriages_divorces/life_expectancy.html

Vaillant, G. E. (1977). Adaption to life. Boston, MA: Little Brown.

Vaillant, G.E., & McArthur, C.C. (1972). Natural history of male psychological health. Seminars in Psychiatry, 4, 415-427.

Van Manen, M. (1990). Researching lived experience. Albany State University of New York Press.

Weber, M. (1930). The protestant ethic and the spirit of capitalism. London, England: Unwin Hyman.

Welch, J. (1982). Spiritual pilgrims. New York, NY: Paulist Press.

Williamson, E.G. (1939). How to counsel students: A manual of techniques for clinical counselors. New York, NY: McGraw- Hill.

A little bit about Dr. Craig Nathanson

Dr. Craig Nathanson is an honorary lecturer at the University of Liverpool, England.

He is also one of the first faculty members for Roehampton University Online, London, England.

Dr. Nathanson has been teaching on-line graduate and undergraduate programs since 2003 and currently is teaching Management programs at Keller (Devry), US.

Dr. Nathanson has been an adjunct faculty member since 2001 at Cal State East Bay in California (USA) teaching in the areas of Management, Leadership, and Human Resources.

Dr. Nathanson is a visiting lecturer in China and Vietnam in partnership with Solvay Brussels School of Economics, Brussels, Belgium, and Benedictine University, US.

Dr. Nathanson worked over 20 years in various senior management positions in U.S. fortune 50 companies and was one of the original founding members of Pandesic, the joint venture of Intel-Sap as one of the first e-commerce companies as well as a vice-president of People PC, a joint venture with Ford Motor Company.

In addition to Joyful Work in Midlife: The five stages, Dr. Nathanson has written and published 4 other books on work and mid-life development and management including "How to find RIGHT work during challenging times" and "The Best Manager: Getting better results through people".

Dr. Nathanson is also a motivational speaker, vocational coach for mid-life adults, executive coach, and organizational consultant working with companies on the development of their organizations and people.

Dr. Nathanson has a Ph.D in Human and Organizational Systems from The Fielding Graduate University in California as well as Masters Degrees in Human Development and Telecommunications Management. Dr. Nathanson's current research focus is on humanistic management, leadership through coaching, and mid-life professional development. Dr. Nathanson developed and leads a thriving online community at www.drcraignathanson.com.

Craig lives with his wife Natasha and family in Petaluma, CA, USA

Dr Craig Nathanson

PO Box 2823

Petaluma Ca 94953

707-774-6446

www.drcraignathanson.com

craignathanson@gmail.com

Watch the Dr. Nathanson You Tube Channel!

http://www.youtube.com/user/thevocationalcoach